Out of Darkness Megabook

Ruth Price

This is a collection of the first three parts of the Out of Darkness series, the serialized novel Out of Darkness, consisting of Out of Darkness #1, Into the Light and In God's Hands. If you enjoy this book, feel free to look over the other titles in the Out of Darkness series.

Published by Global Grafx Press, LLC. © 2013

The Pennsylvania Dutch used in this manuscript is taken from the Revised Pennsylvania German Dictionary: English to Pennsylvania Dutch (1991) by C. Richard Beam, Brookshire Publications, Inc. Lancaster, PA 17603

Copyright © 2013 by Ruth Price
All Rights Reserved.

No part of this publication may be reproduced in any form or by any electronic or mechanical means, including scanning, photocopying, or otherwise without prior written permission of the copyright holder, except by a reviewer who may quote brief passages in a review.

ISBN-13:
978-1494484781

ISBN-10:
1494484781

DEDICATION

This book is dedicated to my grandmother Carolyn who gave me the strength and wisdom that has been a foundation for my life. God bless you in heaven.

CONTENTS

Acknowledgments   I

Out of Darkness #1

Chapter 1   1

Chapter 2   7

Chapter 3   14

Chapter 4   22

Chapter 5   27

Chapter 6   31

Chapter 7   40

Into the Light

Chapter 1	48
Chapter 2	51
Chapter 3	59
Chapter 4	63
Chapter 5	70
Chapter 6	75
Chapter 7	79
Chapter 8	83
Chapter 9	87

In God's Hands

Chapter 1	91
Chapter 2	100
Chapter 3	103
Chapter 4	107
Chapter 5	113
Chapter 6	117
Chapter 7	122
Chapter 8	129

ACKNOWLEDGMENTS

First, I offer all thanks and honor to God Almighty who gave me life and the ability to create. Second, I want to thank my family for their support, especially my dear husband Harold who has put up with the ups and downs of my journey to become a writer. Third, I thank my publishing company, Global Grafx Press, who without their support I wouldn't be seeing my name in print. You're the best!

Out of Darkness #1

My flesh and my heart may fail, but God is the strength of my heart and my portion forever. --Psalm 73:26

CHAPTER 1

Though the rain had stopped, a gentle breeze rustled through the forest canopy, dripping large drops onto the damp earth below. Moonlight peeked through breaks in the thick clouds as owls cried, spiders wove their webs, and a woman slept, collapsed on her side against a tree like an abandoned doll. She had run her socks black and bloody. Her blouse was ripped. Blood seeped from a wound on her temple, matting her hair. Eventually the intermittent fall of water on her face stirred her to wakefulness. She groaned, wiping her eyes with her hand. Her mouth was dry. Her feet and head hurt.

The woman sat up. "Hello!" she shouted, and the dull echo of her own voice frightened her. Maybe she'd been in some sort of camping accident. She tried to summon some memory of the campsite, what friends might be looking for her, but nothing came. She needed help, she knew that. She felt around the ground for her shoes. Where were they?

She wanted to go home, but where was home? She tried to call up memories of her family, and her heart pounded as she realized she had none. She didn't even know her own name. She had to know her name.

It's a run-down room with the windows boarded shut and the only light a bare bulb on the ceiling. In the corner next to the bathroom sits a damp mattress, atop it a dirty sheet. When she is alone, she can hear the rats skittering in the walls. She is not alone now. She stands in front of the mattress, a metal tray clutched in her hands. Though she can't see the man's face through the stocking that masks it, his attention lingers a touch too long. In his waistband, he has a gun. If he comes too close, she can hit him with the tray, but even if she knocks him out, how would she get out of the room? Still, it's her only chance.

He drops six cans of beans on the floor. "Here's your dinner," the man says, his voice a cruel jest. "Don't eat 'em all at once."

Dizziness overcame her. She leaned forward, gripping at the exposed root of one of the surrounding trees and dry heaved. Was that a memory or a dream? The sky had begun to brighten, false dawn or true, she had no idea, but once the dizziness passed, she knew she had to get moving again. The trees loomed like hulking brutes around her, and the rustling of the leaves whispered that whatever she'd run from was still out there.

She stood, drawing her arms around her chest to ward off the chill, and walked. Sticks and small stones stung through her socks. She walked through the chatter of birds that heralded dawn, and as the sun climbed, the air warmed and the trees thinned. When she reached a narrow road, she stopped, hoping and fearing that someone might be there. It was empty. She scrambled down the hill to the road on her rear and crossed the thin stream of tar. In the bright sunlight, the lump of terror behind her ribs began to loosen. If she could just find someone with a phone, she might be able to contact the police or a hospital and get help.

The woman scrambled up another hill and down again. Walking in the heat had brought the dizziness back, and she often had to stop to close her eyes and catch her breath. Her mouth felt dry and filled with cotton. She couldn't imagine ever being so thirsty or so dirty. Her cream colored blouse felt smooth and expensive, and her jeans were cut well for her body. Her nails, though dirty, were even and polished in light pink. She didn't seem the sort to allow herself to fall into disarray.

The forest gave way to fields of green corn. Breeze rustled through the rows, carrying the scent of manure. The whisper of the corn soothed the woman, and for a moment she simply stared, captivated by how the sun kissed the fields in golden light. Beyond the fields stood a large, white farmhouse with an enclosed black buggy parked beside it. Odd, the woman thought, the buggy instead of a car, yet somehow the antiquity of it made her feel safe. She walked towards the farmhouse. As she got closer, she caught sight of a neglected tangle of plants and flowers. A garden! Ripe tomatoes hung from the vines, making the woman's mouth water. She could devour them whole. The thought of their sweet juice on her tongue brought on another wave of dizziness. She closed her eyes and leaned against the side of the farmhouse.

A dog began to bark. It was a Labrador retriever, having been asleep next to the stairs and hidden by the overgrowth of tall grass between the garden and the stairs.

"What's that, Johanna," A man yelled. He emerged from behind the barnyard, striding towards her. "We have a guest?" Spotting her, he waved, "Excuse me, ma'am, are you lost?"

His accent was strange, vaguely German, and the woman asked herself how she could recognize this, how she could know the taste of a raw tomato on her tongue but not remember her own name. "Yes," she answered, opening her eyes and turning towards the voice.

He was tall, dark haired, with a full brown beard that touched his collarbone. The beard made him look older than he was, but his skin was smooth and his eyes glinted with a blue that rivaled the bright summer sky. He wore simple clothing: solid pants with suspenders, a white shirt, and a black, brimmed hat that he took off and held at his side as he faced her. He smiled with a stiffness that made her wonder about a deeper sadness, but the smile looked good on him, softening the severe cast of his cheekbones and his forehead. His eyes widened as he looked over her disheveled appearance, and said, "Ma'am, dear God, you're hurt! What happened to you?"

"I don't..." She didn't know. How could she explain to this strange man that she had no idea what had happened to her or even who she was. He might think she was lying, that she was some kind of criminal.

He took a step towards her, his palms up. "You need the Englischer police and a hospital, ja. But I'll have to take the buggy up to the Millers to use their phone. Come in and let me help you."

"I just need some water," she said, backing away. "I'm sorry. I don't know where I am. You don't have to call anyone." The panic had made her dizzy again, and the fields and farmhouse seemed to spin on an axis around her feet. "I don't feel so good," she said, leaning against the farmhouse again. It desperately needed a painting, she noted, as her guts threatened to rebel.

"I promise, I won't hurt you. Can you walk?" he asked, offering his arm. He stood still, neither approaching nor retreating, and she realized in his steady calm that he meant no harm. She leaned on it, leaned on him, grateful for his solid strength. He smelled of sweat, wool, and something earthy. She breathed it in, steadied by the scent of him as much as his well-muscled arm as they walked together up the wooden stairs into his home.

Sun streamed through the windows of his home. It seemed too large for only one person. They passed through a living room, with two large wooden sofas with plush, green cushions that looked simple and comfortable. The walls were bare wood, finished to a pleasant shine. Sun poured in through a skylight above, and gentle breezes fluttered blue and green patchwork curtains at the windows.

"Please sit," Abram said, leading her to the sofa framed on either side by the windows. Looking through the screened windows, she saw the tangled garden and sprawling fields.

The woman folded her arms protectively over her chest. It was impossible to reconcile the damage done to her body and the smoke of her nightmares with this spacious, airy home and the beauty of nature that surrounded it.

Abram placed his hat on the sofa beside her and strode further into the house. While the home certainly seemed lived in: the dark green throw rug in the center of the floor was frayed a bit about the edges, yet there were no photos or knickknacks on the surface of the end-tables, and neither photographs nor artwork hung on the walls. A set of tools hung on wooden hooks on the far wall by the door, giving some indication of Abram's work or hobbies, and there was a simple straw mat in front of the entrance for wiping ones shoes.

Abram came back less than a minute later with a cool glass of water and sat down on the second sofa, perpendicular to hers and closer to the door. The woman drank the water to the bottom, relishing in the sweet coolness as it washed over her tongue and down her throat. Abram was silent as she drank, only waiting until she had placed the empty cup in her lap to ask if she wanted another.

"Thank you," the woman said awkwardly through the lump of gratitude in her throat. He returned with a second cup and a plate with food: a hunk of what looked like home-baked bread coated in jam and sliced tomatoes. She devoured the food, licking salted tomato juice from her fingers before sipping at the second cup of water.

When she had finished, he asked, "What's your name? My name is Abram."

The woman shook her head. "I don't know."

"You don't know?"

"I don't know anything that happened." She kept the dream of the cruel man and his ring to herself. He might not even be real, some fiction or amalgamation of trauma and her own imagination. "I think I hit my head pretty hard because I don't remember much. I mean, I can talk, and I remember normal things, like that this is a sofa," she pointed, "and that is a window, but aside from a few flashes, I really don't remember anything about myself."

It sounded so farfetched, when said out loud, that she expected Abram to laugh or to claim that she was lying, but instead he simply nodded. "You've suffered something that is clear. I'll need to take the buggy down to the Millers to use their phone to call the Englischer authorities, but you can take a bath in the meantime, and you'll need some clothes."

"Thank you," she said again. She couldn't imagine the picture she presented in her torn clothes, disheveled hair, and muddy socks. The bruise on her head hurt, as did her wrist, which was also bruised with a long scratch as though she had torn herself from someone's grip.

"I...umm..." Abram stared down at his hands, body extraordinarily still. "My wife's should fit you."

"You're married?" Her stomach fell in a feeling of disappointment, which was completely ridiculous because she'd just met the man, not to mention the fact that she might have a boyfriend, or even a husband back in her previous life. Well, probably not the latter as she wasn't wearing a ring. And glancing at his left hand, neither was he.

"Rebekah, she passed on three years back with our son." Abram's tone was flat, but the tension in his broad shoulders, the forced stillness of his features, and the rapid blinking of his eyes hinted at a grief just beneath the surface.

"I'm so sorry," the woman said. She wanted to take his hands to offer some form of comfort, but the thought of standing and breaching the aura of silence that surrounded him seemed too forward. He truly was a handsome man, and the pain he suffered only sharpened his attractiveness, and how horrible was she to even think such thoughts of a man who had helped her even as he bore this terrible pain?

"We cannot alter God's will," Abram said. He rolled his shoulders back and forced a smile that seemed more tragic than the honest display of sorrow. He held out his hand for the cup, which she handed him, and then stood. "Let me show you how to operate the tub. We have plumbing from the diesel generator, but it can run cold after a while. I generally bathe on Sundays, after our church meeting, unless I have a particularly dirty day in the fields or with hauling the furniture I've built for sale."

Abram led her through a kitchen brightly lit by sunlight streaming through a far window. The kitchen had clearly been meant to be a family center, and much of that expectation remained in the layout of the room. In the center was a table with a blue and white patterned tablecloth, around it six wooden chairs. The chair closest to the window was pulled out slightly, and the floor beneath it scuffed as though it was often pushed in and pulled out again. The other chairs, in contrast, had a light layer of dust over them. A gas lantern hung over the table, as well as above each of the two wooden armoires. To the woman's left was a long counter, at the end of which sat a white, humming refrigerator. In the sink sat two pots. The stove was gas and well maintained, but more dust clung to the handle of the oven, and a cobweb had blossomed from the back of the refrigerator to the far wall.

Abram walked to the sink and placed the cup inside. "I apologize for the mess," he said. "I wasn't expecting company, and I haven't even hosted a church service since..." his lips tightened, then he took a breath and continued, "Without a woman in the house to supervise the cooking, well, it's a bit of a challenge, though I rather like preparing simple things, and my sisters and their children bring me baking once a week in exchange for repairs."

"Seems lonely," the woman said, the words spilling out without her thinking. She couldn't imagine how difficult it must be to live alone in a house that had clearly been meant to be shared with love and the expectation of many children to add noise, brightness, and life.

Abram shrugged. "Come this way. We have a regular flush toilet also. I can't tell you how many Englischers act as though we Amish have no amenities at all just because we choose not to connect to their electrical grids."

"You don't have electricity?" But how does the refrigerator work?

"We use generators," Abram explained. "For the basics, but we don't believe in progress for the sake of progress, nor do we hold with the idea of acquiring for the sake of showing ourselves better than our neighbors, which is often a byproduct of your modern conveniences. All of these things distance one from nature and a true relationship with our God."

"Okay," the woman said. She wondered if the person she had been, the person she couldn't remember, had a relationship with God or wanted one. It seemed peaceful, lovely even, to call such a tranquil place home. Rebekah had been a lucky woman.

They passed through the kitchen to a bathroom. It was large, and again lit only by sunlight at this hour, though a gas lantern did hang above the sink. The tub was a steel, claw foot tub and deep, like a Western movie, thought the woman. Had she enjoyed Westerns? As Abram explained to her how to turn on the hot water and to fill and drain the tub, she tried to recall some titles and scenes. Shane? Old Yeller? Something with Mel Gibson and playing cards...

"We'll let the tub fill while I just get you some clothes, ja."

The woman stood to follow, but Abram said, "No, you watch the tub and turn it off when it gets about three-quarters filled."

"Thank you," she said again, the words inadequate to express the riot of feelings which blew like a storm behind her ribcage. Gratitude, lingering fear, confusion, sadness, and a feeling of being drawn to this stranger. As the thud of Abram's footfalls receded down the hallway and into another room, the woman found herself feeling very, very alone.

CHAPTER 2

It was Friday, and Abram Yoder awakened as the dawn sun kissed through his windows. He slept in one of the guest rooms, as he had for the past two years since his wife had died. Abram had entered his marriage room twice only: to air the place after storms and to make sure that the roof and walls were sound. He hadn't cleared Rebekah's clothing from the armoire which he had built for her as his gift for their marriage. Atop their mattress, the quilt she had sewn was now gray with a layer of dust as dulling as the grief of her passing had made his world.

Every morning, Abram reminded himself that Rebekah's death in childbirth had been God's will, as much as the rising of the sun and the flourishing of the fields; a loss he couldn't understand. but with God's aid would someday be able to bear, but most days the prayers lay empty on his lips and in his heart. He was angry at God, though it was foolish to be angry at God - but more than at God, he was angry at himself for allowing his wife to die. She'd been sickly towards the end, ill in the mornings though the time for illness should have long passed, and weak, as she willed herself up to do the household chores, baking and cleaning their clothes by hand. Nothing he said or did would convince her to be less than her perception of the perfect wife, no matter how he'd pleaded with her to rest, that he would take their laundry to one of the Englischer laundries and have his sisters do the baking, as they did for him now. He should have taken her to one of the Englischer hospitals, instead of following her wishes and allowing her to birth at home. The midwife even had advised Rebekah to give birth in a hospital, she'd told Abram later, but Rebekah had insisted she could do it herself.

Every morning, Abram woke in a narrow single bed, and, keeping his eyes shut, he imagined that Rebekah might wake again next to him, slip her arms around him and whisper in his ear that the flowers and cows had awakened, that the baby was up and kicking in her belly, and that the Lord ordained that she and Abram shouldn't lay lazy in bed as well, while there was bread to be baked and furniture to be carved. He imagined her cream skin, the beauty of her smile, how her light brown hair slipped from its plaits in the middle of the night to hang in tendrils about her round cheeks and her glinting green eyes. Of course, when he opened his eyes, he was only discovered the weight of the aging Labrador retriever Johanna dozing on his feet. Except for the dog, Abram was alone to dress, alone to tend to sowing and reaping, alone to care for the mare Ruthie, alone to sit on his steps and force shapes from wood, alone to listen to the whisper of God in the corn and wonder how he might have saved his wife from her own good intentions.

Abram reflected every morning on how his life had changed since Rebekah's passing, and he did so again this morning, before allowing his mind to return to review the arrival of the strange Englischer woman. He had been in the barn, leaving Johanna to doze against the stairs as he fed Ruthie her grain before leaving the horse out to run in the field behind the house, when Johanna began to bark. Catching a glimpse of his visitor, he'd assumed at first she was a tourist who had somehow gotten herself lost, perhaps injured the tires of her Englischer car or had it lose power somehow, and was now in search of a telephone or some other form of assistance.

"Excuse me, ma'am, are you lost?" As he walked closer, he realized from her disheveled appearance, her torn clothes, lack of shoes, and wound on her head that she had fallen into far larger trouble than mere vehicle trouble. She stared at him, her eyes wide, pupils large, and a quiver in her full lips. So he approached her the same way he'd approach a skittish horse after a storm, slowly, palms out, and speaking in low, soothing tones.

Thus he managed to get her into the house, watered, and fed. He sat himself on the second couch as she ate, as was proper, feeling strangely proud as she devoured the simple lunch of buttered bread and tomatoes he'd prepared for her. She was pretty, in the Englischer way: her dark brown eyebrows sculpted and her hair a wavy auburn falling to her shoulders. Her trousers fit her far too well, accentuating the shape of her hips in a way that Abram found embarrassing. He was a married man, though Rebekah had passed on. It was hardly proper for him to ogle this poor woman clearly in need of Englischer assistance.

She didn't even know her own name. That seemed fantastic, even for an Englischer, but the hunch of her shoulders accompanied by the fear in her gaze as it flitted towards Abram then towards her hands, as though she expected he might disbelieve her and put her out made him feel only more protective. He wanted to help her, whoever she was, in the way the Lord intended that man love and help his neighbor, no more. He was far too broken for more, especially with an outsider.

When she had finished eating, Abram showed her to the bathtub, noting how the nameless woman's curious gaze flitted over his kitchen as they passed. She needed clothing. If it wasn't that his own clothing would have been falling off of her, not to mention that he hadn't done laundry for close to two weeks and was thus on his last set of clothing himself aside from what he wore for Sunday services, he would not have considered his wife's clothes. He left her to watch the tub, an excuse more than anything, and ventured for the first time in three months into his and Rebekah's shared bedroom.

He stared at the door of the armoire where her clothing still hung, afraid to open it. It was foolish, her clothes were sewn fabric and nothing more. Rebekah would never have hesitated to offer her clothing to a stranger in need. She would have been ashamed at his hesitation. Rebekah had always been so much stronger than him. Stronger in her faith, stronger in her compassion, truly the best of them both.

Please God, give me strength, Abram prayed. There was no change in him from his prayer. His chest was still congested with sorrow, and the room, for all the brightness of sunlight streaming through the twin windows on either side of the bed, still seemed gray, clogged with the fog of dust and memory. With stinging eyes, Abram opened the door.

Rebekah's clothes hung, hand-sewn plain clothing in greens, blues, and brown. They were solid colors and none too bright. The armoire had protected them from sun damage, and Rebekah's stitching was strong. Rebekah had been well known for her sewing skills. Even before she was married to Abram, her older sisters had sought her out to make baby and childrens clothes because the durability of her work as well as her ability to make patterns which were both plain and yet somehow beautiful placed them in high demand. Rebekah's clothing would suit this lost woman's frame, Abram assumed. He chose one outfit in dark green, which would suit her dark brown eyes. Not that such things mattered before the Almighty.

Closing the armoire quickly, he took the pile of clothing back to the bathroom. His guest would have to make do with her own underthings; no amount of human charity would allow him to offer her Rebekah's without her permission, which she no longer had the ability to give, but at least the rest of her clothing would be clean and modest.

When Abram returned to give her the clothes, she was standing in front of the small mirror in his bathroom that he used for brushing his teeth. She had her thin fingers raised to her cheek. She had conformed to the Englischer standards of grooming. Her brows were shaped and her nails, though chipped, had been manicured in a French style. Her eyes, though large and framed by thick, brown lashes, were set a bit close for true beauty, and her skin lacked the tan of most of the plain women of his community.

"Are you remembering more," Abram asked, clutching his wife's clothes to his chest a bit too tightly.

The Englischer woman shook her head. Her lips were tight, and there was tension about her eyes. "Nothing," she said. "It's like I'm looking at a stranger."

"I'm sorry." Abram handed her the bundle of folded clothing. "Excuse me," he said, backing away once she had taken it.

She thanked him, and listened intently to his instructions about the soap and shampoo, discount brands from the local town store, good enough for him though Rebekah had preferred floral scents, and left her to her business while he went to prepare the buggy and Ruthie for the five mile ride to the Miller's. They would arrive a few hours before dark, enough time to make a phone call and have dinner there while they waited for the police to arrive.

Abram prepared the buggy by rote, his mind engaged with the mystery of who this woman was and what had happened to her. Not that he would have cause to know, truly. Once the damage to her head and heart had healed, she would begin to remember who she was and return to her own world. It was foolish to think differently, that he might somehow hold onto her, a stranger even to herself. He had just finished hitching Ruthie to the buggy when the woman came out. She stood on his deck, barefoot like a true Amish woman except for the halo of hair that hung damp around her face. "Have you any shoes?" she asked, pointing towards her feet. "I wear a size eight. Also, what should I do with this?" in her left hand, she held up the dark green hair covering that Amish women wore to show their respect for God.

For a moment, all Abram could do was stare. This woman looked nothing like Rebekah, aside from the clothes she wore, but that moment, framed in the afternoon sun, as she stood there in Rebekah's clothes, it was for an instant like his wife was back. Abram lowered his gaze and tried to school his expression to some form of propriety. The mix of joy and grief that blew through him like a storm wind had robbed him of his words. He wanted to take her hand, press it to her lips, to court her, except of course that was insane. He had been too long alone, Abram decided. It would be better for him to put an advertisement in the circular, or let his sisters know that he was again ready, discretely, to search for a second wife.

"Shoes," he said. Rebekah's feet had been slightly larger, if he remembered, but with socks they would do. If it had been deeper summer, he'd have just had her go barefoot, as he would have as well for working in the fields, but once the afternoon warmth dulled, the late spring night would be too cold for comfort, especially for her soft, Englischer feet. "Come with me, I'll find you something. And we wear the head covering to show our respect and love of God. An Amish woman would wear her hair in two braids, but you aren't Amish so you should wear it as you like." He hoped she wouldn't decide to wear her hair Amish style. It would be too much, less like she was borrowing his wife's clothes and more like she was becoming something akin to the woman who had inhabited them. "Yes, just keep it loose so it dries," Abram added. "The buggy is ready. You should bring your old clothes, just in case the police need them for..." he waved his hand. "Whatever reason it is they might need them. Stay here, I'll get you shoes."

It was easier this time, entering the bedroom, rummaging through the dresser for socks and beneath for Rebekah's shoes. The socks had been darned by Rebekah's mamm. While Rebekah had talent for sewing, she'd declared herself two left hands with knitting of any kind. When Abram returned, the Englischer woman was sitting on the stairs petting Johanna. The dog had rested her head on the Englischer woman's lap, Johanna's eyes half closed in contentment as her tongue lolled from her mouth.

"I'd best see her fed before we leave," Abram said. He'd carved a dog entrance in the back door, so she'd be able to enter and leave as she liked, though she generally preferred the barn when he wasn't home. He put out her food while the Englischer woman put on the socks and shoes, drawing the laces tight and wrapping them around her ankles twice before tying them to keep them in place.

"It will take half an hour to reach the Miller's." Abram said as they walked to the buggy. "You may sit inside if you like."

"Where will you be?"

"Guiding Ruthie, up front."

"May I join you?"

"Yes, of course."

Abram offered his hand to help her onto the front of the buggy before climbing himself. When they had both settled, he took the reins in hand and used them to stir Ruthie towards the road. "Good girl, Ruthie," he said, nickering encouragement towards her.

The Englischer woman laughed. "You have a way with animals."

Abram shrugged, a bit embarrassed at her attention. The buggy seat was narrow, which meant that they had to sit closely, hips touching. She didn't appear to notice the closeness, but of course she wouldn't. Englischer culture allowed for far more casual touching between men and women, rendering such closeness meaningless. Even with her memory lost, her instincts would lead her to think nothing amiss.

They rode past his fields onto the road. It wasn't a main thoroughfare, and while tourists often came to Lancaster to take photos of the Amish and taste their food at Amish style restaurants, this area was a bit too removed for most to venture. Abram was grateful for that. He didn't like the presumption of the Englischers with their cameras, as though his choice of how to live was somehow quaint, worthy of an afternoon of superficial gaping with no thought to the reasons or humanity of the person inside his or her plain clothing. But the fascination with their lifestyle brought the community much needed customers which helped support the elderly and those who needed medical care.

After a few minutes on the road, the Englischer woman asked, "Where are we?"

Abram's face heated, and he was grateful for the partial cover of his beard. She didn't even know her own name, how could she be expected to understand where she was? "In Lancaster. Do you know it?"

"Yes, I've seen commercials," her eyes widened and her voice took on a greater excitement. "I remember the TV. It was a box type, in color, and we had a cable box underneath it. And a hardwood floor with a red rug. It smells like...garlic...yes, someone's cooking, but it's not me." She was silent for another minute and then said, "It's gone. I wish I could remember more."

"It will come back to you, as God wills," Abram said.

As they approached a turn in the road, there was a rumble behind them. Ruthie, a generally placid mare, twitched her ears backwards at the noise. The Englischer woman shifted on the bench, twisting her body towards the sound. Abram nudged Ruthie closer to the side of the road in order to allow the car to pass. At the bend, the road was narrower than Abram would have liked, and the car, one of the Englischer mini-vans, was large and wide.

It was a problem Abram was used to, but as the mini-van whipped around the corner at a much faster pace than the slow plodding of the buggy, his passenger's breath caught. "Was that close?" she asked.

Abram smiled. "I've seen closer. Don't worry, ma'am, Ruthie is a calm horse. Not much rattles her."

"Well, I'm glad of that. And your capable driving."

Abram couldn't help but smile. They passed the rest of the time in pleasant conversation as Abram did his best to give the Englischer woman information about the neighboring farms, land, and those who lived there. He was well behind on the neighborhood gossip, having always counted on Rebekah to fill that gap, but his fragments of knowledge seemed to fascinate her, and the trip passed quickly.

As Abram slowed Ruthie to make the turn into the Miller farm, a number of other buggies were already parked, and a crowd of children ran up to him. Abram recognized three as the Miller's two youngest sons and daughter, and a few of the other faces as neighboring families, but three were unfamiliar, as were two of the buggies and the car. Abram's skin went cold. He'd never liked crowds, and he hadn't dealt with so many people at once since his wife's funeral. Especially not strangers. Abram's grip tightened on the reins as he tried to steady his breathing.

"Is everything okay?" the Englischer woman whispered.

"Fine."

"Abram!" the oldest of the Miller boys, Emmanuel, walked alongside the buggy. He was barefoot in plainclothes like the rest, but there was something about his way of standing with his thumbs in his waistband that lent him an air of dishevelment no matter how well his mamm sewed and ironed his clothes. He added, breathing heavily at the light jog he had to use to keep up with the buggy, "Did you come for the Singing Circle? We're hosting this week."

"That's for young men. I've well passed my rumspringa," Abram said. "We're here to use the telephone, that's all. This Englischer stranger needs to make a phone call.

"Englischer!" Emmanuel raised both straw colored eyebrows. "How is it..."

"Just take me to your Daed or Mamm. This is adult business."

"Right! You can park Ruthie right next to Mr. Price's buggy." Emmanuel pointed to his next youngest brother Isaiah. "Tell mamm Mr. Yodel's brought an Englischer woman to use the phone. She's in the kitchen finishing up the baking for the singing circle."

Isaiah nodded and then took off at a dead run, his untucked shirt flapping in the breeze as he ran towards the large farmhouse.

CHAPTER 3

Michael Maglione believed in getting a little bit extra. He'd only buy a mattress if they threw in the sheets, he never left the bank without an extra pen, and he always took fistfuls of hot mustard with his fried rice, even though he had a drawer of it next to the knives in his kitchen. When Mike took a job, he got it done, but he was always careful to take his cut. So when Carl asked him for a favor, Mike agreed readily. He owed the man, and locking some spoiled rich kid in a Lancaster cabin for a few days was hardly a challenge. Besides, if the girl was cute, he might even get a bit extra.

The first day, Mike and another guy, rail thin and sweaty who only went by D, sat watch in front of the door of Sofia's room. They took turns bringing in her meals. The farmhouse Carl had appropriated was one step from falling in and way too hot. The girl, woman actually and wearing a nice sized diamond on her left hand, got the only working toilet in the place. The rest of them had to go out into the woods and squat like animals hugging a roll of Charmin'. This didn't put Mike in a good mood. Worse was the fact that Carl had a real stick up his you know what, and wouldn't let them so much as look at the girl in a lustful way.

"Rule one," Carl explained with all the gravitas of a TV lawyer, "You don't damage the goods. Scare is alright, but nothing that leaves DNA, got it?"

So Mike kept his eyes on and hands off, a real challenge considering how the heat had forced Sofia to unbutton her blouse almost to her nipples and roll her pants over her knees. They'd taken her shoes, of course. Hard to run without shoes.

Carl monopolized the TV, which wasn't much of a loss as it was a box from what looked like 1993 that sometimes turned the characters on the screen green and sometimes froze up when the signal stuttered. And because they were running incognito, it was canned beans and peanut butter and jelly. By the end of the first day, Mike was about ready to lose his mind from boredom. There was only so much Sudoku a man could do. D entertained himself with a knapsack full of legal thrillers, which frankly seemed ridiculous considering their occupation.

"Gotta educate yourself, man," D said, when Mike questioned his literary taste.

D took first watch, and Mike the second. He was just getting ready to shake D awake when Carl said, "I've got to go out and get the paper. Make sure she gets her breakfast and uses the toilet. I don't want any complications."

"Yes, sir."

Mike did as he was told, putting the stocking over his face to protect his identity before stepping in, tray of reheated eggs and beans with two slices of white bread in hand. He allowed his gaze to linger a bit longer than was polite over Sofia's soft curves as he handed her the tray. Her eyes and nose were red from crying, and her bed was rumpled only at the edge farthest from the door, where she had clearly slept atop of the blankets, curled in a small ball, her head resting on the pillow. Her hands shook as she took the tray. "Why are you doing this?"

"Money," Mike said.

Unshed tears brightened her large hazel eyes. "But my money is in trust. It can only be used for education until after I graduate college!"

"Not my problem," This was one of the things Mike hated about kidnap jobs. He didn't know why these people insisted on trying to explain their entire life story to him. He didn't care, and if he had, he wouldn't be able to do much. Even supposing her hard luck story somehow softened his heart enough to let her go, that would put him in big trouble with Carl and whoever had employed Carl. Mike liked his knees and thumbs thank you very much.

Mike said, "You'll need to eat that and use the bathroom."

Sofia's lower lip quivered as she twisted her engagement ring around her finger with her opposite hand. "Or is it Daniel?"

"That your fiancé? He give you that rock?"

"Yes."

"Could be, since he's flush with money. I don't know for sure. They just pay me to watch the door."

She bit the inside of her lip, then took a breath. "How much do you want?" she asked, running her hand over her hair.

"Excuse me?"

"I'll give you this," Sofia held her hand out to him, the ring twinkling in the light of the bare bulb above. "It's worth five grand, at least. Just take it and let me go. I haven't seen any of your faces. Just look the other way, give me a half hour, and I'll be on my way."

Well, at least this one was more interesting than most, but no matter how much he wanted the ring, Carl would *crucify* Mike if he let his charge escape. Literally. "Sorry," he said, handing her the tray. "Not interested."

It rained off and on throughout the day. Carl didn't return, and after a few hours, Mike appropriated the television, turning the volume up as high as it would go and angling the screen towards the hall so that if they sat at the end of it, they could see the left half. Mike tried Carl's cell-phone throughout the day, but it only rang and went through to the message machine. After a couple of hours, D excused himself to piss in the woods, and when he came back a half an hour later, he said, "There's a room full of costumes on the second floor."

"You went up those stairs? That could have killed you."

"I held the railing." D shrugged. "Anyway, they have a couple of cop outfits, and a fireman, and an EMT..."

"And an Indian, right?"

D blinked. "No, but there were some army uniforms, and one SS officer, though that one's got moth holes in the crotch."

"Fascinating."

At noon, D gave the girl lunch and Mike took the dinner shift.

When Mike closed and locked the door behind him, D said, "We're running low on beans and marshmallows. When'd Carl say he was getting back?"

Mike shrugged. "He said he was going out for the paper so's he could make the video, but he ain't picking up his phone."

"Think he got caught? Cops could be on us."

"Carl? Not likely." But a cold lump settled in Mike's belly. "I been calling him. It's a burner cell."

"Cops can track that stuff, man. Haven't you ever seen Law and Order?" D pushed the paperback he was reading into his knapsack. "We've gotta get out of here. And wipe down our prints."

"And the girl?"

"Dunno, just leave her there. Cops'll let her out." D stood. "Where's the paper towels? And you'd better take the gun. We'll wipe it clean and put it in the river."

Mike began to pace the hall, avoiding the hole in the floor just before the living room entrance. "Carl'll kill us if we run."

"I'm not going to jail," D said. "I promised my girl I was done doing this shady stuff. She won't visit me in prison, man."

"We don't know he's been caught."

"Either that or he ran. Either way, cops is onto us. They're closing in, could be outside now. You need to lose that phone. Take the battery out for now, then we'll throw it away with the gun."

This job just got worse and worse. D had a point though. It didn't take nine hours to get a paper, any more than it was taking Mike's dad 22 years to buy a pack of cigarettes. "We'll give the girl the rest of the beans," Mike said. "In case the cops is slow."

"Fine. But you'd better use the rubber gloves so's you don't leave prints. Can't do nothing about the hair and skin."

"Man, you're as paranoid as Carl," but D's agitation and Carl's absence had put a worm of fear into Mike. He hadn't signed up for a stint in prison.

Mike placed the gun in his waistband and went to the kitchen to look for a pair of gloves. The floor was cracked off-white linoleum that lead to a red, barely functional gas stove, though rust had settled on the oven handle and the area around the burners had a rim of brownish-black burnt oil residue. D had scrubbed the counter, though some dirt remained in the cracks. An eighteen-roll pack of toilet paper sat on the edge of it, next to the refrigerator, which hummed and coughed loudly. Above the counter were two cabinets. One was missing a door. Inside, Mike found a half used roll of paper towels and a dust covered spray-bottle of industrial bleach. Now where were the gloves? Mike wiggled the drawer beneath the counter to get it open. Inside were five mismatched gardening gloves with flower patterns. He put on a pair. They were tight on his hands, which immediately began sweating.

Mike took the other three to D. "Pick your poison," Mike said, handing them over.

D grimaced. "That's the best you could do?"

"You go ahead and search if you think you'll do a better job."

"Uh-uh." D took the bleach and paper towels and started to scrub down visible surfaces. He went at it with gusto.

"I'm gonna take these beans in for the girl," Mike said. "And the bread." If the cops took too long, and she starved to death, and then they found Mike, that could be a charge of murder on his head too.

When Mike entered the room, Sofia stood at the far corner in front of the cot, the tray gripped in her hands. "What's going on?" she demanded.

"Here's your dinner," Mike said, dropping the six cans of beans in a pile on the floor. "Don't eat it all at once."

Sofia took another step towards him. "My name is Sofia." She was crying now, God help him. Mike preferred it when they bargained, or even better tried to offer him sex. "Please help me. I haven't seen your faces and I won't say anything."

"Are you going to offer me your rock again?" Mike pitched his voice low.

"Do you want it?" Sofia asked.

"Yes." It was the least Mike could get for a job gone so horribly wrong. "And a feel." Because it was important to get a little bit extra. Especially if

Carl did blame him for running, which he would, Mike didn't kid himself. He'd have to tell Carl the girl had overpowered him somehow. With the bullet-proof glass of a prisoner's visiting room window between him and his employer, Mike might live long enough to make that explanation.

"What do you mean, a feel?"

"You've got a nice rack," Mike said, "Now put the tray down and come here."

There was a knock at the door.

Mike shouted, "Not now, D."

"What's taking you so long?"

"I'm fine!"

Blessed silence. "Hurry up," Mike whispered to the girl.

Sofia stood a moment, grasping the tray and shaking. She was prettier when a bit afraid. The shaking made her lady-bits wiggle, and she looked at him with proper respect.

"Now." Mike ordered.

Still clutching the tray in the crook of her right arm, Sofia pulled at the ring and once she'd twisted it free, said, "Open the door."

"What?"

"I give you the ring, you let me go, that's the deal. So open the door."

This was getting annoying. Mike said, "You give me a touch, and a taste if I'd like. I take the ring, and I don't shoot you. That's the deal."

Sofia burst into tears. She clutched the tray to her chest as though she imagined it might stop a bullet. "No."

"What's going on in there?" D shouted through the door.

"Nothing!" Mike shouted, and then added in a hissed whisper that he hoped in his annoyance sounded properly threatening. "If you don't, I'll take what I want and strip the rest from your corpse."

Sofia screamed.

There was loud click as D unlocked the door and rushed in. He had a bat in both hands, his head craning back and forth around the room like a seagull pecking at the air for food. "What's going on?!"

Before Mike could respond, Sofia threw the ring. It flew in a glittering arc between Mike and D, smacking the far wall with a light tap before falling to the floor. Mike's gaze followed it, his attention in that split second focused away from that little bit extra, as Sofia shoved past him at a dead run.

Mike made a grab at Sofia, catching the sleeve of her shirt, but she yanked her arm away with shocking strength and careened into D's side. D brought the bat down, grazing her temple, and she stumbled. Mike dove towards her. The gun clattered free of where he had shoved it into his pocket and skidded across the ground. A ferocious bang sounded as the gun discharged, which froze Mike and D in place.

D let out a string of curses. Mike looked down at himself, afraid he'd been shot though he felt no pain.

"She's getting away!" D shouted. He took off down the hall after her. After a moment, Mike followed. Sofia made her way down the hall, through the living room and out the door, which had unfortunately been kept unlocked for easy access to the outside. Sofia avoided the driveway leading to the main road, and instead dove into the cover of the weeds and trees which had overtaken what had once been fields. The sun was setting, and in the twilight, her white shirt fluttered between the trees. Mike overtook D across the patch of cleared land. For a skinny guy, D was a terrible runner, and Mike had easily overtaken him. D's face was red, hands on his knees, he gasped, "Asthma."

Mike didn't have the breath to curse. He caught sight of Sofia again, scrambling up an incline into deeper woods. Mike strode after, his breath wheezing in his chest. He didn't like running. Mike had a body for slow motion bar brawls, solid and large enough to take a hit or five before knocking a guy on his back with one motion of his large, powerful fist.

Inside the canopy of trees it was dark, with only hints of the twilight peeking through the leaves above. When Mike made it up the incline, Sofia was only about eighty feet ahead of him, and slowing, lucky that. If she'd been wearing dark colors, he doubted he'd have been able to see her at all. The incline had ascended to a narrow strip of trees and rocks bordering a sharp drop into what looked like an overgrown valley that Mike guessed had once been a dried creek bed. Patches of rocky ground were visible through the thick vegetation. Mike also had to slow to keep himself from falling on the uncertain ground, but even with her adrenaline and the mud softening the ground beneath her, her lack of shoes made the rocky terrain more difficult and soon he had surpassed her pace.

Sofia must have heard him coming up from behind, because she gave a half scream, half whine and managed a last push of speed. Mike took in a deep breath and ran faster. He grabbed at her arm, his fingers whispering over her flesh as the rocky dirt beneath her feet shifted and gave. Her arms wheeled, grabbing at anything, but falling rocks had caused her to topple forward. Mike grabbed at her, cursing. Then the ground beneath him began to move, and Mike backed away as the side of the hill rushed downwards in a mini-avalanche of mud and rocks.

Sofia screamed once and then was silent. When the rock fall had ended, Mike leaned carefully over the edge. Sofia was there, about fifteen feet down, unmoving, against a tree where she had fallen. "Well," Mike said, wiping the sleeve of his shirt over his forehead. He stared a bit at the body, seeing if she would get up and try to run again. His t-shirt was soaked through with sweat and while the air had cooled somewhat, the air was thick and humid, promising more rain.

Without climbing down the steep incline, Mike had no way to determine whether she was alive. The question was, should he risk his neck scaling down this treacherous hill face to see if the girl was dead? And what would he do if she wasn't? Drag her back up? No, he didn't have to be D to know that dragging around the injured, possibly dead woman who he'd run into a ditch wasn't a good idea. Call an ambulance then? As if anyone would buy that he'd just been walking in the woods when he stumbled across an unconscious kidnap victim, even if she never woke up to tell her story and then identify him from his voice.

Then, as a sign from above, it started to drizzle, the large intermittent drops which always came before a heavy storm.

Sofia's dead, Mike decided. He'd take the ring from where she'd thrown it in the room, if D hadn't gotten to it first, pawn it, and move West. They had need of a man of his services on the West coast. And there'd be starlets and wannabe starlets all eager for a taste of excitement and a strong, older man. Or at least that's how they showed it in the movies.

Mike was halfway back down the hill towards the farmhouse, having tripped over two tree roots, stubbed his foot on a rock, and gotten bitten by about fifty mosquitoes when D came jogging and wheezing out of the waist high weeds which surrounded the farmhouse. "Mike, did you get her?" D clutched Mike's prepaid phone, which was ringing Pachelbel's canon in his left hand.

"She's dead," Mike said.

D's eyes widened, making him look like a startled ferret. "That's not good, Mike," he said, rapid-fire. "Not good. We're in so much trouble!"

"Who's on the phone?"

"Dunno, they called ten minutes ago, but when I called back it said Lancaster General hospital. Whoever it was left a message."

"Did you check it?"

"Police can track that stuff, man."

And they couldn't track D calling the hospital? D's paranoia could get to be a bit much. Besides, the mention of the hospital brought a horrible, alternate suspicion for Carl's absence. They'd rented the car with cash, and Carl had filled out a bunch of paperwork. Had he listed Mike somewhere as an emergency contact? Mike had gotten his license at eighteen, but never bothered with cars more than that. It was easier and cheaper to bum rides off of people, so how would he know how car rentals went. But if Carl hadn't been caught by the cops, if he'd gotten into an accident instead...

"Give me the phone," Mike said.

There must have been something in his face, because D handed it over without argument. Mike flipped the phone open and listened to the message.

"What's wrong?" D asked, when Mike had ended the call.

"Carl's been in a car accident," Mike said. "He went into surgery at three."

"Will he make it?" D asked, nervously rubbing his hands together.

"God I hope not," Mike said.

But since the Atlanta job, God had gotten out of the habit of answering Mike's prayers. In a perverse way, it was one of the few things in this world that made Mike a believer.

CHAPTER 4

Abram's hand was warm and a bit damp as he offered his arm to help the Englischer girl onto the buggy. The dress he'd given her was a bit long, and she had to roll up the sleeves and hold up the hem in order to walk around. She couldn't imagine how difficult it must be for Abram to see her, a stranger, in his dead wife's clothes. Still, she was grateful for the bath and to change into something clean. She rather liked how the dress fell over her body. The cut wasn't flattering, but it was comfortable, and she felt somehow safer to be swathed in these layers of cloth, as though the men from her nightmares might look past her if they saw her. She could breathe.

In fact, only her hair felt out of place, though she had no idea what to do with it nor how to properly cram it under the head-covering. She also admired the color of the dress, a rich, leaf green which suited her. She wondered if Abram had chosen it for that reason, though that presumed a greater attention to her looks than seemed likely considering his at most neutral attitude of helpfulness towards her. And to be honest, the woman hadn't any idea what she would do with that attention if it was focused on her. She wasn't sure of her culture or family background, but in her bones she knew it was very different from his.

She climbed up onto the front seat of the buggy and he followed. The buggy was narrow, so they had to sit with their legs touching. It was only a casual touch, born of necessity, but it solidified a connection between the two that hummed with an unspoken significance. Abram deftly guided the horse onto the road, the steady clomp of her hooves as much a comfort as the rattling buggy beneath her and the solid competence of Abram's hands.

"You have a way with animals," she said.

Abram only shrugged, his gaze focused ahead, his cheeks a bit pink either from embarrassment at the compliment or from the sun. His modesty, his quiet attention was intoxicating in its way. Not that she had any business holding such thoughts about this man. She had to get herself together. She shouldn't put so much meaning into a simple expression or touch. It wouldn't be fair to her or Abram, who had already lost so much. Soon, she would learn who she had been and return to her own life, whatever that was. She'd best get started on that now, instead of weaving fantasies from sunshine.

"Where are we," she asked, hesitantly.

"Lancaster," Abram's cheeks had definitely darkened now. "Do you know it?"

And she did, a flash of memory as vivid as it was fleeting. She let the words spill from her mouth, trying her best to capture it before it faded. Her home had been large and beautifully kept with hardwood floors similar to Abram's but finished to a brighter shine. She remembered the smell of garlic cooking and a plush red carpet. Unlike Abram's, her home had electric lights, and there had been a hum behind the television, a fan of some type or possibly an air-conditioner. The images hung in her head, vivid and golden, shining like a Christmas angel. But no matter how hard she tried to recall more, a face, a name, it all faded. "It's all gone," she said. If only there had been more, something to give her some indication of who she was.

"It will come back to you, as God wills," Abram said. The platitude should have angered her, but in the face of his great loss, it was difficult to disparage the strength of his faith. In truth, it awed her, that Abram could continue to live by the laws of and pray to a God that most people, in his position, would assume had abandoned him. Whatever her past life, she doubted her own faith had been so true.

When the rumbling of a car sounded behind them, the sound was both jarring and frightening. Ruthie barely twitched her ears. The woman found herself shrinking toward Abram as he held steady to the reins, allowing the car to pass in a way that seemed far too fast and far too close. For the rest of the ride, he entertained her with stories about the fields and people of the farms they passed. As he spoke, his voice became more animated. He spoke with quiet love of the land and his community. Some of the stories, such as the egg thieving chicken, made her laugh out loud and even brought a chuckle to Abram's lips. He looked much younger when he smiled. It seemed too soon when he turned off the paved road onto a dirt road leading to another large, white house surrounded by a well-kept and flourishing garden.

A swarm of children ran towards them. In their plain clothes and faces red from running, it was difficult to tell one from the next, but Abram quickly struck up a conversation with one of the oldest, a straw-headed boy named Emmanuel. It occurred to the woman, as she accepted Abram's arm to guide her down from the buggy, that she would likely not be riding back to his farm with him. Once the police were called and she returned to her old life, she wouldn't have any reason to pay call to Abram again.

They followed the gaggle of children into the Miller's home. Their home was even more sprawling than Abram's two story home, but the bustle of women and men, children and teens filled the home with an energy that seemed cozy and alive. Inside the main living room sat ten teens. They were basically dressed in Amish style, though one of the boys had a hole in his left ear pierced, and another of the girls had hair which was clearly dyed blond. They looked to range in age from about sixteen to their early twenties. The boys and girls mingled, speaking to each other in low tones with animated hand gestures.

As her gaze lingered, Abram explained, "Rumspringa. It means running around time. This is when a young man or woman has a chance to experience the outside world, should they wish. It's also when they find the person they will marry. After that, they will choose whether or not to be baptized and join the Amish church."

"What happens if they don't?"

"Then they are shunned and must make their way outside of the community. There are many temptations to the modern world, but most of us choose to remain here and live a life of faith."

"Did you do rumspringa too?"

"Yes, Rebekah and I both, though I was a good deal wilder than Rebekah. If it wasn't for her, I might have chosen differently."

The door opened and another pair of young men came in. The first was tall and thin, reminiscent of a scarecrow with blond-brown hair combed into barely manageable tufts behind his ears. He wore narrow glasses and smiled with a chip in his front tooth. His friend, who seemed to be college age, if not older, was classically handsome: broad shouldered and dark haired with green eyes reminiscent of pine needles. His grin was almost perfect, excepting a slight crookedness to his top teeth which seemed more endearing than problematic. Both men were clean shaven. "Mamm," the dark haired man said, "We're here for the circle. And who is this?" He approached the stranger and held out his hand. His grin demanded attention, and the stranger found herself smiling back. He said, "It's lovely to meet you. Are you here for the circle as well?"

"She's an Englischer, here to use the phone, Samuel," Abram said, taking a step closer to her side. "She won't be staying."

"I believe the lady can speak for herself," Samuel said. "Might I have the privilege of your name?"

"She doesn't know. Stop interrogating her."

"Grace," Samuel said.

"Excuse me?"

Samuel took her hand. "It's only by the Grace of God then that we have met."

"Samuel." Abram's voice was harsh. "Manners."

Samuel's grip was brief, her hand barely resting in his, but the warmth in his eyes was genuine and exciting as their gazes met. "Until you remember your true name, I will call you Grace. I meant no offense."

"Grace," the Englischer woman rolled the word on her tongue. She liked it. Maybe it had been her real name, though she sensed no familiarity in it.

"Come along, the telephone is in the hallway," Abram said. "We'll need to get you back to your people."

"Yes, of course." Of course she should want to go to her own home, wherever or whatever that was. Yet the largest part of her wanted to stay here, immerse herself in the warm community of family and friends that had gathered here. Glancing over at Abram, his features seemed set, and there was a tightness to his shoulders. Of course, she had been a trouble to him. And he didn't seem the sort to like large groups of people, considering the quietness of his home and life which she had disturbed. She had imposed enough, taking his wife's clothes, forcing him to come here out of a sense of charity.

"Abram!" Mrs. Miller ran out from the kitchen, her son Emmanuel following behind. "I'm so glad you came. It's good to see you out and about, not cooped up in that large house all to yourself." She was a round woman, not fat, but round in the face and arms, with two thick, dark brown braids framing her apple cheeks. Her brown eyes widened as she saw the Englischer woman. "You! You're the one the Englischer police were looking for!" Her gaze rested on the bruise on the woman's temple. "Oh dear, what happened to your head?"

"I don't know," the woman said.

"She doesn't know anything about herself," Abram explained. "Not even her name."

"You forgot your own name!" Emmanuel exclaimed.

"Shhh! You'll be frightening our guest. The officer left me a phone number to contact him at in case one of us found you," Mrs. Miller wiped the flour on her hands onto her apron. "Your mamm and daed are quite worried, the officer said."

"Did he say anything else?" the woman asked.

"He said you were from Philadelphia and gave us a description of you. He said your name was Sofia Angelis, I wrote it down with the number, here, come with me."

"Sofia." She said it aloud, trying out the feel of it in her mouth. The name was no more familiar than Grace had been. Two names, and both of them strange.

Emanuel's outburst brought the attention of the other youths to the stranger, and some of the teens and young men and women, gathered for the singing circle, began to come over to them. "Mamm," a girl who looked to be about seventeen asked, "Who is this?"

"An Englischer in need of help," "Come with me, miss." Mrs. Miller took Sofia by the arm and led her to the hallway where a black telephone was mounted against the wall. It was a simple touch tone, with no caller ID. On a cork board above the phone was a smattering of coupons with phone numbers. One handwritten note was pinned on the far left corner, away from the others. It read, "Officer Maglione" and a phone number that began with a 267 area code.

Mrs. Miller dialed the number and held the phone up to her ear. The voice on the other side was muffled. Mrs. Miller nodded once, and again. "Ja, ja," she said. "In twenty minutes, that sounds good. Yes, the poor girl looks like she suffered a pretty sharp knock on the head and doesn't seem to remember anything about herself. Ja. We'll see you soon, Officer. Ja. Thank you."

Mrs. Miller hung up the phone. "Best you join with the others for the Singing Circle. I bet you're hungry. Abram lives off of canned food and whatever baking his sister manages to hustle over to him. You must be starving."

"I am." The woman, no, she had a name now, Sofia, swallowed down a painful lump in her throat. Soon, she would find out who she was and maybe what had happened to her. Soon she would be safe.

"Oh!" Mrs. Miller took her arm. "It must be such a relief, I can't even imagine."

Relief, yes, it had to be. But the thread of fear that had faded in the warm sunshine of Abram's home and the quiet strength of his presence now wove cold tendrils through her guts. It was irrational, as irrational as being a stranger in her own body. She, no her name was Sofia, forced a smile. "If you don't mind, I'd love something to eat, and thank you Mrs. Miller."

"Annie," Mrs. Miller said, their arms still tightly interlaced. "Call me Annie."

CHAPTER 5

The accident had totaled the car, fracturing Carl's hip and causing a shard of metal to puncture a hole in his large bowel, the latter requiring immediate surgery in order to prevent sepsis from killing him. Mike had left the nurse with instruction to have Carl call him back when he was able to use his phone. Then there was the problem of what to do about the girl.

"We should run," Mike said. "Before they let Carl out. Go West."

"I have a girlfriend. I can't leave her. Who knows what Carl will do to her?"

Mike knew exactly what Carl would do, unfortunately. "Take her with you."

"You've never seen Janine pack. Takes her the whole night for a weekend in the Poconos. No way am I getting her to pack up her life in that same time. No way."

None of which was Mike's problem, except now that he'd made the suggestion to go West, D knew about it and would certainly relay that information to Carl either in an attempt to bargain for his life or with the assistance of hot metal slivers under the fingernails.

"Hmm..." Mike murmured. Canada was also an option. Or maybe the Dakotas, as much as he hated the cold.

"Besides, we don't have any money."

"Hmm..."

"I mean, we could pawn that girl's ring and split the profits, but I'm sure it's a custom job, and if the cops are looking for her, which they must be, or they will when they find the body at least, they'll use that and the video from the pawn shop to track us down and then we'll be on the block for murder." D sighed.

For a second, Mike was furious. "How'd you know about the ring?"

"Oh, she tried to give it to me so I'd let her go, but you'd have to be an idiot. Everyone knows the cops track that kind of stuff."

Mike was tempted to ask D how someone with such a deep and abiding fear and respect for the law had turned to a life of crime, but that would be getting personal, and Mike didn't mix personal with business. Not unless it would get him something, preferably laid. He did have a point about the ring though. Rich people marked their stuff, and for something that special, they'd have it in every database. Even if Mike tried to sell it, even to the jewel guy he knew on fifth, it'd come up for sure. Without the money from the ring, Mike had about fifty dollars in his bank account, and maybe another ten dollars change in his couch. With that, he'd be lucky to get a bus ticket to Ohio. Panic seeping into his skin, Mike asked, "What are we going to do?"

"That's what I was asking you."

The options were pretty straightforward. Lie to Carl and die horribly when he found out or tell Carl the truth and hope enough begging would lead Carl to mercifully only beat them within inches of their lives. Mike said, "We have to tell Carl she escaped and got herself killed. And bury the body, at least enough to keep the cops from finding her straightaway. And throw her ring in the woods, but nowhere near the gun."

"Where's the body?"

"Up the hill and keep walking. There's a sharp drop off on the other side. Did you see any shovels around this place?"

"Let's look." Mike put the phone down on the kitchen table and they went through the house, one dim flashlight between them, until they found a rusted coal shovel in the basement. When they'd gotten back upstairs, the message light was blinking on Mike's phone. Mike held the phone to his ear. Of course, it was Carl. His voice was as strong as ever as he said, "They're keeping me in this godforsaken hole until Monday morning. There's a general store about three miles away on foot." Carl gave directions to it and to where he'd hidden a container full of money to pay for essentials, as he'd put it. He finished with, "Anything happens to the package, and I'm taking it out of your flesh. With interest."

Mike listened to the message twice, and then ended the phone connection. "We're going to have to run," Mike said. "Carl left some money in the house."

"What about the body."

"Forget the body. Carl's gonna kill us when he finds out we lost the girl. Do you want to be here for that?"

"Are you sure she's dead? It's more difficult to feel for a pulse than how they do it in the movies."

"I didn't feel for any pulse," Mike said.

"Then how do you know she's dead?"

"She was caught in a rock slide and dropped like fifteen feet onto some rocks. She wasn't moving. I think I heard her neck snap." The last was an exaggeration, but Mike knew what a dead body looked like. There'd been his grandmother at the home, and that one drug addict who had frozen to death scrunched against the dumpster behind his apartment three winters back.

"But you didn't check?"

"I wasn't going to get my footprints and DNA all over there as well," Mike added, hoping he'd managed to keep most of the sarcasm from his tone, "Cops can track that stuff."

"Still, we should look," D said, his face lighting up in a relieved smile. "If she isn't dead, then we'll just drag her back and put her in the room again."

"Where she can finish up dying here instead of where we left her?" Mike didn't wait for a response. "We should find the money first. And go first thing in the morning, so there's some light. Otherwise one or the both of us may be joining her." Not to mention the rain, which had gotten heavier, beating against the roof and dripping through the holes in it down onto the floor.

"If she's alive, we can't just leave her out there. It's not right," D said. His narrow face was damp, and he pinched at his forearm as though trying to wake himself. "I didn't sign on to actually kill anyone. We're just supposed to watch the door."

"And if the parents or boyfriend didn't pay up, what do you think would happen to her then?"

"Have you ever killed anyone?"

"Today," Mike took a breath as he remembered Sofia, the body, crumpled against that tree. "But it wasn't my fault. She's the one that ran."

D clapped a hand on Mike's bicep. "Don't worry man, she could be alive. Let's just go look for her, and bring her back here okay?"

"Fine." Tramping out into the woods in the rain to bury a body was not how Mike had planned to spend his evening. But now he wondered. What if she was alive? What would his grandmother say if he left her out there in the rain? Truthfully, his grandmother would have approved of few of his activities. Then again, she hadn't approved of any of his girlfriends either, even the ones who hadn't been strippers.

A ferocious crack of thunder sounded above. Then the sky outside the window lit to white, and the television shut off. Outside, the rain fell even more strongly.

"But not now," Mike added. "No point in having three bodies up in these woods."

"Three bodies?" D said. "Bet there's already more than three bodies out there now." But he didn't argue. Together, as one, they searched the house by flashlight to find the tin of dollar bills that Carl had hidden in a loose floorboard under the sofa. It took almost until dawn for the rain to slow.

Mike and Carl shared a tin of beans and then, shovel in hand, trekked on up the hill.

The girl was gone.

"This is good, isn't it?" D asked, clapping Mike just above the small of his back. "You didn't kill her. You must be so glad!"

"Oh, yes," Mike said, his teeth grit. "That's a load off the mind. Now all we have to do is find out where she went and get her back before she tells the cops what happened. Not to mention when Carl finds out. It's much better this way."

In the corner of Mike's vision, D nodded. Mike had a few ideas of what he might have done in his life to deserve this, what he couldn't figure was how D had managed to live this long without developing any sense for sarcasm at all.

CHAPTER 6

Seeing that Samuel had decided to stop disgracing himself by imposing familiarity upon this stranger in the eyes of the Lord, and that he had put the Englischer woman safely into Annie's arms, Abram went back to the buggy to retrieve the tattered clothes Sofia had been wearing when she stumbled onto his doorstep, mere hours ago. It was settled then. Sofia would return to her people, and Abram to his home. Had there been any other outcome?

In truth, Abram had no reason to stay any longer. Annie would see that his wife's clothes were returned to him, at some point. It wasn't as though Rebekah needed them any longer. Truthfully, he should offer them to the community at the next Church meeting. Rebekah wouldn't appreciate his hoarding her things. It was wasteful and Rebekah had abhorred waste. Yes, once he had returned the Englischer woman's clothes, it would make the most sense for him to be on his way before dark. Not that he feared the roads in the dark any more than he would in the day. But, tomorrow morning, he had to wake early to take his furniture to the auction. There would be many Englischer and Amish customers who might buy the set of four chairs he had finished yesterday.

When he returned, Sofia was sitting at the edge of the group who had gathered for the singing circle. Samuel had taken a seat next to her, his friend on his opposite side. The boys had yet to take their vows to the Church and marry, and as such they were all clean-shaven, even Samuel, though at a week before his 24th birthday, he was past time to have decided whether he would marry and join the church or leave the community forever. Though Abram would never speak his thoughts on the subject out-loud, he found Samuel's waiting to be a sign of frivolity rather than thoughtfulness. With a foot in each world, he enjoyed the best of both, and he was far too handsome by half.

Shocked at the rancor of his thoughts, Abram closed his eyes briefly and prayed, *Dear Lord, protect me from the sin of envy, that I might better serve you and my fellow man.* Taking a calming breath through his nose, he started towards Sofia. He should bid her farewell. It was the least he could do. And tell her not to worry for the clothing. Rebekah, in the grace and beauty of heaven, would certainly understand.

The youths were already singing in the main living room. It was large enough to seat the twenty youths who were seated on the sofas and wooden stools that had been brought out for the occasion. Singing circles at the Millers were more spontaneous than most, Abram remembered. Sometimes the youths would sing for fifteen or twenty minutes at a stretch, one starting a song immediately where the others left off, punctuated by laughter, jokes, and applause. Other times, as much as a quarter hour could pass between songs as the youths socialized, formed community bonds, and preferably settled on someone as a mate. After an hour or so, Annie and the other women would come in with large trays of food: sweet breads, sliced tomatoes, potato salad, and moon pies for the young men and women to devour, calling an official end to the singing. Most were homeward bound soon thereafter, though Annie usually ended up opening her guest rooms for a smattering that were too far flung or too tired to take the long journey home.

Sofia had been given a place of honor on one of the sofas, sharing it with one of Annie's oldest daughters, a sixteen-year old named Miriam. Samuel had pulled up a stool on Sofia's other side, just far enough away to stay in the bounds of propriety. Barely. He sang quietly, his attention clearly split between the proceedings and the pretty Englischer girl.

They made a good couple even with her falsely colored hair. Abram suspected Sofia was in her early twenties, though her Englischer style of personal grooming made her appear subtly older. Or maybe it was the wariness with which she sat, sharing only hesitant smiles with Samuel, her hands folded tightly in her lap and ankles crossed. Her face lit when she saw Abram however, and she gave him a bright smile as she waved him over. A feeling of lightness came over Abram as he walked towards the Englischer girl. She trusted him. He had barely crossed the room before he began to chastise himself for taking such pride in this simple gesture. Of course the Englischer girl trusted him. She had known him longer than the others.

He took up an empty stool, pulled it to Samuel's other side and waited for the hymn to finish. Samuel sang softly, and a bit off key, which sent a stab of venomous joy through Abram. What was wrong with him? His sister had said grief too long held would fester, and perhaps it had. Abram joined his voice, a strong baritone, in with the others. It had been a long time since he'd had the chance or impetus to sing, but though his voice was rusty, he sang the notes true.

On his rumspringa, Abram had sung with a local band, and though putting one's self forward to raise oneself above others was a sin under the Ordnung, he'd loved being on the stage, drawing joy and excitement from the listeners below as they jumped, danced, and applauded at his efforts. That high had been stronger than the drugs other members of the band had taken, a chaotic lifestyle which had led to constant infighting in the band and its eventual implosion. The high of performing had been second only to the joy of holding his wife, her belly fluttering against his palm as the baby kicked. At that time, he could sense God's voice in the whisper the wind over the cornfields, in Rebekah's warm smile and soft breathing, in her feet woven between his as they slept.

There was a smattering of applause and then the low murmur of conversation while people decided what to sing next. "That was lovely," Sofia said, when Abram sat beside her. She leaned towards him. The shortness of the stool meant she didn't have to look up to meet his eyes. "What language is that? German?"

"You have a good ear," Abram said. "Most people would have assumed Dutch, I suppose because the Englischers have named Lancaster as Pennsylvania Dutch Country for the tourists."

"Thank you," Sofia pushed a stray hair back behind her ear. "You're all so kind. I hope I can pay you back someday for all the help you've given me."

"Helping your fellow man is required in the Ordnung and a tenet of the Bible as well. There's no need to thank us."

"Yes, Abram is the picture of a proper Amish man," Samuel cut in. "He's to be admired." Samuel's words and expression seemed kindly meant, but something in the steadiness of his gaze made Abram doubt his sincerity. Foolish man, Abram chastised himself again. Abram was acting like a smeeli himself, a youth just turned sixteen instead of a man. How could Abram allow himself to become jealous of a child's flirtations with a stranger who was leaving them in less than a quarter hour? Samuel couldn't help his good looks and facile way of speaking any more than Abram could the power and range of his voice. A man was given talents to use for the glory of God. So long as he did not use those talents to place himself above his fellow man, or succumb to the mirror sins of pride and envy, only good could come of it. Abram needed deeper prayer, perhaps a conversation with the Bishop about this corruption that threatened to make inroads on his soul.

"No matter how we try, labor, it is easy to fall from grace," Abram said seriously. "So, have you settled on a particular woman to court?"

"I don't want to get ahead of myself," Samuel said. "I have prayed long and hard, but the Lord has not yet seen fit to let His will be known to me. Or perhaps I don't yet know how to properly listen. How did you know?"

"Excuse me?" Abram's immediate reaction was white hot anger, immediately quelled in shame. He had been drawn to Rebekah from their first conversation, him in Philadelphia for his band, and her at the Reading Terminal market selling baked goods. Though they'd both been born and raised in Lancaster, she'd been clear on the other side of the district, and if their paths had crossed prior to that meeting, it had made no impression on either of them. She had been only seventeen, him twenty two, and they'd been baptized and married a year later. He often questioned the speed of their courtship, if it would not have been better for her to have had a better taste of the world, not that she'd wanted it. Rebekah had been content with their farm and their life. So had he, until the end.

Sofia laid a soft hand on his. "Are you okay? You don't have to answer. It can't be easy for you."

"I knew from our second conversation, and suspected from our first. At that time, God whispered so easily in my life."

A knock sounded at the front door. It could only be the police officer, Abram thought, here to take Sofia away. "Don't worry about the clothes," Abram said. "Take them as a gift to remember your time here."

"Thank you," Sofia said, her voice thick.

Ruth stood and ran to the door. "One moment!"

The angle of the room to the hall meant that even as close to the room's entrance as Abram was, he could only catch a partial outline of the officer's frame. He could hear well enough, as the ambient conversation in the room silenced, all listening while pretending they weren't actively eavesdropping as Ruth greeted the officer. The officer had a distinctive accent, as though he'd lived in a different part of the country before coming to Pennsylvania.

Sofia's grip on Abram's hand tightened, squeezing painfully.

When Abram turned his attention to her, Sofia's face had lost all color, and she was hunched over herself protectively. Abram whispered, "What's wrong?"

Sofia was shaking, her entire body; never had Abram seen someone so afraid.

Ruth yelled, "Officer Maglione says he's here for the Englischer. Where is she?"

"No. Please no," Sofia whispered.

"Take Sofia through the back hall to the kitchen and out the back. She can stay at your place for the time being." Abram ordered Samuel, dislodging her hand and placing it in Samuel's. The words came without thought, as though given directly from the mouth of God. Samuel nodded, and led Sofia from the room.

Abram walked to the door to confront the police officer, hopeful that the Lord would continue to guide his steps, that he might say the right thing to keep Sofia safe. Whatever had happened to her was brutal enough to leave her bruised in flesh and hollowed in spirit, and her fears, whether rational or not, deserved proper consideration.

Officer Maglione was whipcord thin with stringy light brown hair that brushed the top of his ears. He wore a badge, and a billy club and a holstered gun hung from the belt at his hip. His walkie-talkie was silent, possibly turned off out of respect for Amish custom. He looked up as Abram approached, his eyes at first shining with the same anticipation of a cat stalking a mouse before blinking, a flash of confusion crossing his features, "Where's the girl?" he asked, looking over Abram with narrowed eyes.

"Ruth," Abram said, waving towards the girl who had opened the door. "Annie needs you in the kitchen to help with arranging the breads for after the circle, please."

Ruth thankfully left without questioning how Abram had come to know this.

"The girl," the officer said again, a bit louder.

Lying was a sin under the Ordnung, the vow by which Abram had chosen to live his life when he was baptized before his marriage. While he had often failed to measure up to the task in spirit as well as letter, he had not, until this point, deliberately chosen to defy it.

Dear God, Abram prayed, *please guide my path and my tongue that I might be a vessel for Your will.* He took a breath and said, "I don't know where she is. She seemed agitated. I think she left."

Officer Maglione's eyes widened and his lips parted in obvious disbelief. His collar shifted, and Abram caught a glimpse of a fresh scab on his neck, as though some animal had scratched the officer just last night. A vein throbbed in his neck as he asked in a very controlled voice, "Where did she go?"

Abram shrugged. "I don't know. It's Englischer business. We choose not to involve ourselves in Englischer business."

"I'll need to search the premises," the police officer said.

He attempted to push past Abram, who stood firm. "Has this woman committed a crime? Annie said her family was looking for her."

"They are."

"Then I suppose she's decided to return to them. Or not." Abram shrugged again, schooling his expression to stoic blandness. "It's an individual's choice whether or not they return to their parents' world, ja."

The vein in Officer Maglione's neck pulsed faster, and he gripped the base of his club with white knuckled fingers. His knuckles were scratched, with fresh scabs where someone or some action on his part had recently drawn blood. "We have reason to believe Sofia may have come to harm. This is obstruction of justice."

It was perfectly reasonable that the police officer be upset if he believed Sofia to be in danger, and Abram should have simply allowed him to speak with the Englischer girl, if nothing else so she could assure her family that she was safe. Yet something about this man had awakened a fear in the Englischer woman so strong that she had been literally shivering in her chair. And the scratches, on Officer Maglione's hands and neck, where he might have struck someone who in turn had been struggling to escape, roused suspicion in Abram. There was something odd about this police officer. He certainly wasn't local, and his uniform didn't exactly resemble the Philadelphia officers he'd seen either. He should not be allowed within sight of Sofia, and certainly would not have opportunity to take her away if Abram have anything to do with it.

"You have to let me search your house, it's the law."

"This way, officer." Abram said. Not waiting for a reply, Abram started towards the room where all of the others were gathered. By giving the police officer a guided tour, that would hopefully allow Samuel enough time to not only get Sofia out of the house, but also safely hidden.

"Abram!" There was a swish of skirts as Annie came running in from the kitchen. A white splotch of flour clung to her forehead just below her kapp. "Why didn't you tell me Officer Maglione was here? Hello officer, may I offer you something to eat or drink? The Englischer girl is in the main room."

"Your husband said she'd left."

Annie burst out laughing. "Abram! He's the same age as my youngest brother. My husband is at the Deacon's meeting." Her attention turned back to Abram. "What do you mean, left? Where'd she go?"

"She said she remembered something and left with Samuel."

"And you just let her run off into the dark? With Samuel! He's not yet an adult." Annie's expression glowered with disapproval. "Abram Yoder, this is disgraceful."

"I couldn't force her to stay, Annie. It's not our way."

"You're even more rigid than Rebekah! I swear, if the pair of you had even a bit of common sense, maybe she wouldn't ha..." Annie brought her hand up to her mouth with an expression of pure horror. "I'm so sorry. Rebekah was a good and Godly woman. I would never speak ill of her."

Abram was too shocked at this revelation of how his wife had been perceived to do anything but stare. Rigid about the Ordnung? Of course he was rigid about the Ordnung. He'd taken a vow to live his life by those tenets, in order to be closer to God. There was no greater thing to strive for, because in that striving their love for each other, had been as one. He wondered what Rebekah thought, looking down on him from the next life, at his duplicity now. He hadn't lied. God had at least worked through him well enough to avoid the letter of deceit, if not the practice of it. Or was it pride to assume that God was the one guiding him? The road to sin was bricked with the justifications a man made to uphold his own image of righteousness.

Still, God had given Sofia to Abram's care, and he would not let her down.

They walked into the living room. The other members of the singing group were seated on the stools and sofas. They looked up at the Englischer police officer as he entered.

"He's here about the Englischer woman," Abram said. "The one who left with Samuel."

"Did she tell any of you where she was going?" Officer Maglione asked.

There was a round of head shaking. One of the girls said, "Samuel was flirting with her." She was tall with very sharp features and dark brown hair that made her seem more severe than her nineteen years of age. There was a hint of resentment to her tone, and her lip curled on the word "flirting" as though she wished Samuel had saved his flirting for her instead.

"I'm so sorry, Officer Maglione," Annie said. Her round cheeks were red. "I'll certainly have her call you again should she come back. Maybe she has just decided to return to her family. If any of us could get her in one of your English cars tonight, it would be Samuel. I fear he's more out of the Community than in, though as his mamm's only son, he's reluctant to leave her all-together. Whenever you make a choice, there's always a sacrifice."

"Do you know what sort of vehicle this Samuel might be driving?" Annie shrugged. "He's not yet been baptized, so he has no prohibition against using any vehicle he likes. He would have parked it some distance from here though, in order not to be rude. But Abram here heard that she might be going home. Poor thing had lost her memory, though maybe she's gained something back. If she finds her own way home, her family will be just as pleased as if she came in your capable hands. That would be for the best."

"Right," Officer Maglione said, but his expression was fixed, and when he spoke, there was a stress to his tone, as though his jaw was tight with some form of stress. He studied each of the remaining youths at the singing circle with calculating eyes. When he had determined the obvious, that Sofia wasn't there, he asked to look through the rest of the house.

"Sure, if you like," Annie said. Abram stayed at the officer's side as he looked through the house. His gaze flitted to paintings and empty spaces. He even had Annie open the door to her bedroom, something about which she was not pleased. When he had finished his search of the house, he took his leave. At this point, the sweet smell of sugared breads had permeated the first floor. Some of the girls had taken the trays of food from the kitchen and begun to distribute them. Next was laughter and more singing, as the youths hummed with excitement and speculation.

"A bit odd, that one," Annie said, once the police officer was gone. "What did he think, we'd kidnapped the poor girl?"

"Something happened to her. You saw that wound on her head, and the clothes she was wearing before were torn and she didn't have any shoes, only muddy socks," Abram said. "When she heard that police officer's voice, she was terrified."

"Why would she be scared of the police?"

"She wasn't scared of the police. She was scared of that officer specifically. That's why I asked Samuel to take her. She was so scared she was shaking."

"You think that Englischer police officer did something to her?"

"I don't know. I don't think she does either. But there's something wrong about this situation. It was as though God guided my words when I was speaking with that officer. And maybe it's nothing, but I couldn't let her go with him, not when she was so scared."

"Humph. You really are willing to go a long way for a stranger, and an Englischer to boot."

"It's not so much. The Ordnung says that we should help others. "

"Be careful Abram," Annie said. "Even if she wasn't troubled, she would be an Englischer, and very, very young. If you're interested in finding another wife, I will be happy to help. You've lived too long alone as it is. It will be good to bring some light into your house."

"I...I don't..." How could Abram think of replacing Rebekah in his home or in his heart?

"It's just good to see you out for something other than a Church meeting or the like. And this is the most alive I've seen you in a long time. I thank God for bringing the Englischer girl into your life for that. I just hope by God she is safe and will be able to return to her mamm and daed unharmed. Well," Annie corrected herself, "Having suffered no more harm. Are you going to ride home tonight, or do you think you'll need to stay over?"

"I asked Samuel to take Sofia to stay the night at my sister's. I should go also, to make sure she's comfortable."

"Comfortable, ja." Annie pursed her lips. "Be careful, Abram. You don't know this girl. She doesn't even know herself."

"Ja, danki." Abram said, thanking her.

Annie didn't let him go until she had piled up a take home container filled with cinnamon smelling friendship bread and creamed potato casserole. "Just a little something to share with Esther," she said. "You take care of yourself, ja. Take care with your heart."

It was a fair warning, Abram thought. Not that he had any expectations beyond helping the Englischer girl. The man he had been briefly, before Rebekah and his vows to the church, might have been able to cross into her world, but for now, his place was here.

Food in hand, Abram walked past the room where the singing circle was still in full swing. A tremulous soprano coursed over the group, and soon the others joined in. Abram paused at the entrance, leaning against the door frame.

It was a hymn of thanksgiving which Abram had sung all through his childhood, as had all of them, and he sang it with all his heart. No matter how it all had ended, he was grateful to his bones that Rebekah had been his wife. He wished that she had stayed with him long enough for their love to have settled from the newness of passion to the steadiness of true and lasting love, bound together in the eyes of the Almighty. But Rebekah was gone, and she would not want him to mourn her forever. Abram had to move forward, not by leaving her behind, but by allowing her place in his heart to be warmed by God's light. God is love, Abram reminded himself. Yes, he would take care with his heart, but that didn't mean he should hide it. He could not make room for God unless he allowed himself to love again.

CHAPTER 7

"This way," Samuel whispered in Sofia's ear, and then louder said, "Excuse us," followed by something in German.

Sofia could barely think beyond the beating of her heart telling her to run, run, and run. The policeman's voice, the cadence of his speech, was exactly the same as the cruel man in her dream. He would take her back to that place where her nightmares lived, that place that had swallowed up the memories of her true self.

They stood and scooted sideways between the sofa and close-packed stools towards the room's second entrance, opposite the first on the far wall. From there, Samuel led her down a dark hallway and three closed doors. The Miller house was huge and sprawling. Gas lanterns hung along the walls in intervals of five paces, but none were lit. Sofia could only make out their outlines from the bright triangle of light coming from behind her, where the singing circle had gathered.

Walking in the too-long skirt was awkward in the dark, and Sofia stumbled twice, but soon Samuel was turning the knob to another door and outside onto a gravel path banked by garden plants on each side. The sun was setting, painting the sky in orange and red. It was still warm, a bit hot in the dress Abram had loaned her, but fear had put a cold layer of sweat on her skin. She wiped her forehead with the sleeve of the dress. Her kapp hung awkwardly a bit to the left over her loose hair, the edges touching the top of her ear. Samuel put his finger to his lips and held his hand up, motioning her to stop.

Then Samuel left her, ranging out ahead. Alone, protected only by the partial obstruction of the tomato plants winding up a latticework along the fence, Sofia squatted beside the wall of the Miller house and did her best to stay absolutely silent. A breeze rustled through the garden. A bird cried above. Terrified, Sofia hugged her arms around her chest. Did she believe in God with such an absolute certainty as the Amish people who had come to her aid? She wished she could be certain her prayers would have such power, that her faith could hold strong in the face of loss, betrayal and fear.

Dear God, Sofia said in her mind. *I may or may not be one of your believers, but please, if you're listening, don't let him catch me.*

Sofia sat for a time after that, flinching at the movement of leaves, until Samuel returned. He waved her over, and she followed. They skirted the Miller land, going around a green cornfield and a barn before tracking along a narrow dirt road that seemed to run the edge of the property. Samuel set a brisk pace, painful to her in Sofia's too large shoes, but fear propelled her onwards without complaint. They had been walking for close to fifteen minutes when they reached a second, smaller shed, bound by a chain and combination lock. Samuel spun the combination with ease and then throwing the chain over his shoulder, swung the door open.

"Stay put," Samuel said. Inside was a fold out table littered with tools in front of a classic car in mid-repair, with steel bumpers and headlights jutting forward from the front hood like eyes. The paint was a dull green, with the passenger's side door revealing exposed metal, but the tires were new and the hubcaps gleamed.

Samuel walked to the car and placing a hand on the hood, said, "I'm not finished with her yet, though I've replaced the engine and done most of the body work excepting the paint job," He gave Sofia a shy smile. "I got work at a local garage, so I can get the parts at wholesale. Still was a real pain to find a door for a 1940s Oldsmobile."

"You can drive?" Sofia had thought all Amish people rode in buggies like Abram.

"For rumspringa, you're supposed to experience the outside world before deciding whether or not you will stay in the community. I got my driver's license at 18. One of the guys at the garage taught me. I love cars, though I really shouldn't. It would break my mamm's heart if I didn't get baptized and stay here."

"Can't you visit?" Sofia asked. "No matter what, your mom will want to see you."

"I'm her only son. If I leave, I won't..." Samuel's hand clenched on the hood of the car, fingertips pressing into the ancient paint. Though the shed was lit only by cracks in the slats of the walls and a battery powered lamp on the table, "My father died when I was nine. Leaving would feel like a betrayal of everything he taught me of how to be a good and godly man. How can I give that up for a hunk of Englischer metal on wheels?"

Sofia skirted the table and hesitantly placed a palm on Samuel's back. "Your father would want you to be happy," she said. Maybe God's plan for you involves working on cars.

"Maybe," Samuel sighed and rolled his shoulders back. He was dressed in Amish style, black pants, white shirt and suspenders. He rolled the sleeves up on his shirt, revealing well defined arm muscles. "Just give me a minute to get the battery hooked in. I don't turn it on much, so it's better to keep the battery disconnected so that it doesn't get drained if something is left on accidentally. We can take it to Abram's sister's though, once things have settled down, unless there's somewhere else you'd rather go."

"No." Sofia had no idea what to do. She was terrified to contact the police again. That police officer had hurt her, possibly been responsible for kidnapping her in the first place. It seemed unlikely that the entire police force had been involved, but until she regained her memories, she wouldn't know who to trust. Well, she trusted Abram, and Samuel. None of the Amish people who had sheltered her seemed to have any interest beyond helping her. They were good people. "I need time to find out who I am. I have a name at least. Maybe I can go to a library and research more about myself tomorrow." Maybe there would be some sort of missing persons report on her. Some way she could find someone who knew her without running the risk of being threatened again. "But maybe tomorrow or the next day, I could visit a library? I don't want to contact the police again, not without knowing more about myself."

"My younger sister and some others in the community sell baked goods at the Reading Terminal market on some weekdays," Samuel said. "You can ride with them into the city, but the city library won't open until Monday and I don't think they're going until Tuesday or Wednesday. Why don't you join us for Church meeting tomorrow, and I can take you to the Lancaster library on Monday? Someone there should be able to help you with the computers."

"Yes, please!" Sofia said. "If it isn't too much trouble. I don't know what I can give..."

"It doesn't matter. You'll be our guest for a while. A beautiful Englischer lady is its own reward, ja."

Sofia's cheeks grew warm. Beautiful? She had looked at herself briefly in Abram's mirror, mainly hoping to recognize something, but she hadn't considered her appearance beyond that. She was slim, and her hair had been lightened. Her skin was light, and she had a mole on her left cheek. Her eyes were a bit round and brown, her cheekbones were a bit flat, pointed chin and jaw a bit too wide. She had full lips and thin lashes. Her ears were pierced with small pearl studs that felt like nothing in them; she had probably worn them a while to grow so used to them. She supposed she was pretty enough. Beautiful though...no, that had to be more flattery than truth.

Samuel smiled, and his eyes shone in the dull light of the battery operated lamp on the table behind them. "We can stay here for the next hour or so, then go back before the circle breaks up."

"Back?" Her heart beat faster. "Why do we need to go back?"

"Safer to have you leave in one of the buggies. You're dressed plain. All we need to do is properly braid your hair. Anyone watching will just assume you're one of the girls who came for the circle. Hide in plain sight," he grinned. "Literally."

Sofia couldn't help but grin at Samuel's cleverness. "What a great idea!"

He ran a hand through his hair, longish a bit in the front, and said, "Denki." It's nothing though."

"Are the seats done?" Sofia asked. "Inside your car?"

"Ja. Did you want to sit inside?"

"Might be nice."

"No radio yet, though I do have a small iPod. I got used to working to classic rock at the garage. This way, Miss Grace."

She felt she should correct her name to Sofia, but who knew if that was even right? Samuel led her around to the front of the car, outlining the work he'd done on the exterior and engine with an enthusiasm that brought warmth to his handsome features. He moved his hands as he spoke in dramatic gestures, pointing towards this and that like an excited child. When he finally pulled the door open and gestured for her to step inside, she felt as though she'd been given a rapid-fire education on the intricacies of how to repair and maintain a car. It was interesting and fun. Samuel's energy was like fire to the deep calm of Abram's deliberate nature. His energy drew her in a different way from Abram's calm assurance.

She stepped into the car; the seat was smooth leather but the floor was as yet not carpeted, with bits of open space exposing the undercarriage. She breathed in the scent of leather, oil, and iron as Samuel walked around the car and sat in the driver's seat.

"I'm sorry," Samuel said. "I've just been talking and talking at you."

"It's fine," Sofia said. "I like listening. It's clear how much you care for this."

"Yeah, well..."

"It's not a bad thing." Sofia wondered at his religion that would make him choose to abandon something that meant so much to him. "If you decide not to follow Amish ways, what would your family say?"

"Nothing. I mean, my mother would be disappointed, profoundly so, but she would say nothing. I know at this point people think my choice should be obvious. They say I'm simply too afraid or too selfish to make a decision, or that I've already made one. The wrong one. But I do want God to be in my life and for us to have a close relationship. It's just hard to let go."

Sofia didn't understand why he should have to, but she barely understood them so it didn't seem her place to judge. "I think God would want you to be happy," she said.

"Ja."

They sat in silence for a while, listening to the creaking of the wind over the shed and the awakening of the nighttime animals and insects. There was an anticipation in the air, half fear of what might await her outside, and half something more visceral. Samuel was a handsome man. Even in relative stillness, he exuded energy, tapping his index finger against his thigh. He said, "I wish I had something to feed you. You must be hungry."

She was, but she only shrugged. "It's fine." In order to forestall another long silence, Sofia said, "Maybe you should show me how Amish girls braid their hair?"

"I...uh..." Samuel ran his hand through his hair, pulling it at the ends.

Sofia smiled. "I assume there's some method to it. And I'll need something to tie the ends with."

"Hold on," Samuel opened the car door. He went to the toolbox and rummaged around or a bit, until he came out with a spool of white string and a pair of scissors. Balancing them in his left arm, he got back into the car, placed the scissors and string on his lap before cutting off two lengths of about four inches. "I've only watched my mamm and sisters do this, but I think if I do the first part, you should be able to handle the rest."

"Thank you." Sofia removed the kapp and turned in the seat so that her back was to his. "Is that good?"

"Fine," Samuel said. "Lean back a little so I can reach the front." Sofia did as instructed and Samuel placed his fingers at her front hairline, deftly running them in a line towards her neck to create a part. "You're going to have to braid this tightly," he said. "Your hair is a bit short, but it should do I think." He took the first half and combed it gently with his fingers. "Why do you dye it?" he asked.

Sofia shrugged.

"Right, you wouldn't know. But you should stop. Your natural color is prettier at your roots. It's got amber highlights."

Sofia's face heated. She wondered if the blush was apparent all the way to the back of her neck. Thankfully the light in here was dim. Samuel's fingers worked gently through her wavy hair, tugging at the knots. Then he put it into three sections and braided it tightly. He was close, the light spice of his soap or aftershave or maybe just him caressed her nose, just as his fingers gently worked her hair. She closed her eyes, enjoying the languid sensuality of his hands, the gentle movements of the breeze over the slats of the shed, and the caress of the cooling night air.

When he had finished, he handed her a piece of string and asked, "Can you finish the rest?"

Sofia took the string and wove it around the end of her hair, leaving a short wavy curl at the bottom as Samuel finished the second braid. When she had tied the second, she allowed herself to lean back into the chair.

Samuel stared at her.

"What is it?" Sofia asked, touching one of the braids. "Is something wrong?"

"Aside from the eyebrows, you really look plain. No! I mean, like us."

Sofia laughed. "Thank you, I guess."

"No, it's good. You still need to put on the kapp."

Sofia took the kapp from where it had fallen on her lap and placed it on her head.

"No. Like this," Samuel leaned over to adjust it, his fingers brushing her cheeks as he tied it in a bow below her neck. When he was finished, his fingers lingered. He gazed into her eyes, and a tendril of desire curled in Sofia's belly. He didn't make her feel safe like Abram, but she liked his energy, the optimistic way he went about things in spite of the difficult decisions he had to face. Still, she was far too much of a mess to offer him anything. She ran her thumb over the wrist hem of the dress that Abram had given her. Abram's wife's dress, a woman who he had loved so deeply and with all of his heart. Somehow, kissing another man in these clothes felt like a betrayal of that gift. Outside, an owl cried. Embarrassed, Sofia turned her head to look out the side window. "Thank you," she said.

"I'm sorry," Samuel said, settling back into his chair. "I didn't meant to make you uncomfortable."

"You haven't."

"We should get going to my mom's. The singing circle should have wrapped up by now. I'll just explain what's going on and ask if you can sleep in my sister's room."

"Are you sure that's okay?"

"It's a little odd, but she'll listen to me, and she wouldn't put a lady out after dark. Especially not someone in need."

"I can't thank you enough. For everything."

"God tells us to love our neighbor as ourselves and help those in need. Abram might be a bit of a stick in the mud, but he's right about that."

"He's not a stick!" Sofia said, eager to defend Abram. Quiet and steady, certainly, but beneath that, he had a depth that came not only from pain but from a confidence that couldn't be faked. Abram knew who and what he was.

Samuel cocked his head. "Ahhh..." His lips ghosted a smile. "I see."

"What?"

"Well, I've always enjoyed a challenge, ja." Not waiting for a response, Samuel opened the car door. "Are you ready to go?"

"Yes." Sofia said. Not that Sofia hadn't enjoyed Samuel's company. Not that she didn't want to feel his lips on hers. It was all so confusing! Sofia hoped it would all become clear in the morning. Maybe more of her memories would come back, and she'd know what the police officer had done to her and why. All she knew was that he had hurt her.

"Good. I need to get something from the glove compartment, then we can go. Why don't you stand over there?" Samuel said, pointing towards the door.

Sofia did as she was told. Sam leaned over to the passenger's side of the car and jiggled with the glove compartment handle. It took a few shakes before it open, spilling its contents onto the floor. Her view of the fallen contents was shielded by his body, but she noticed that when he stood, something dull and metal was in his lap. It took a moment for Sofia to realize what it might be, but still she didn't believe. "Is that a gun?" Sofia asked.

"I got it at a show. It's a revolver. I've only fired it a few times at the range." Samuel shoved the gun barrel first into the back of his pants.

Sofia was incredulous. She knew that Samuel had not yet joined the Amish community, but she'd thought of him as Amish. She'd never thought of him as dangerous. "Are you sure that's safe?"

"Don't worry, it's not loaded," Samuel said. "I have some bullets in my pocket, but I'll only load it if there's an emergency."

"I don't want you to bring it," Sofia said. As scared as she was of the two men who were stalking her, she didn't want to invite more violence into her new friends' lives. "You should throw it away."

"I'm not going to use it unless there's a problem. Like if those men come around, if they're the ones who attacked you."

"Please, don't," Sofia begged him. She wasn't even sure why she was so set against Samuel having such a weapon. If that policeman, the one whose voice she recognized if only in her fear of it, came back, he would certainly have a gun. Sofia wouldn't be able to resist him without some way to defend herself. But the thought of seeing Samuel with that gun in hand, the blood it would leave on his spirit if he fired it, was too sad to contemplate. "I can't stand the thought of you using that thing. Please, leave it here. Or better yet, sell it and buy something else for your car."

Samuel stood and crossed the shed, cupping Sofia's hands in his. "You are so good. It's in every part of you, a God given light that makes things clearer and more beautiful just for having been shone upon."

"So you'll leave it?"

Samuel squeezed her hands, for an instant tightly enough to hurt. "It's for my family too," he said. "I'll only use it if I have no choice."

As Sofia followed Samuel from the shed, fear settled over her, stronger and deeper than before. She willed herself as best she could to *remember*.

When they reached the end of the field, Samuel said, "Stop." He hopped over a gully and then said, "Take my hand."

It took another twenty minutes to reach Samuel's home. In that time, the best her memory gave her was the smell of damp, a diamond ring, and the muffled ringing of a land line phone. It was ephemeral, so much so that Sofia felt she might have imagined it all in her desperation. None of it measured to the warmth of Samuel's hand.

Into the Light

There is no fear in love, but perfect love casts out fear. For fear has to do with punishment, and whoever fears has not been perfected in love. --John 4:18

CHAPTER 1

It had been D's idea to use the costumes they'd found in the attic, pose as cops and pass the number of Mike's burner cell to the local Amish farms, so that if the girl showed up, someone would call Mike instead of the real police. It was a terrible plan. For one, Mike's bottom was too big for the uniform pants, so he'd had to substitute them with the pair of wrinkled slacks from his backpack. The top of the uniform jacket was also snug around the middle, but at least he could keep that open. D's uniform was even worse, short in the arms and legs and loose in the chest. Yes, using the uniforms was a terrible idea altogether, but the problem was that Mike didn't know a better way to find Sofia or her corpse at least, and if they didn't find it, Carl would skin them both alive with a spoon.

They walked the two miles to the main road, and from there took a right, which Mike vaguely remembered had led to a store of some kind. In the lot, D spotted a 1993 Cadillac. "Perfect," he said, pulling a bobby pin from his pocket. "Keep an eye out."

Because Mike's uniform fit better, he got stuck going door to door. The easy smiles and odd accent of the Amish people made Mike more uncomfortable than the lies he told. People said Amish farms were quaint, which Mike figured was probably true, if quaint meant old and boring at the same time. Life moved too slow here, and the people with their same clothes, hair, and bushy beards, seemed to be hiding some secret. They had their own language, Mike remembered that from the visit to Amish country he'd made with his mother as a preteen. It hadn't been horrible. He'd liked the food, but he didn't get the rest of it. How could those kids look so happy without a Nintendo system in their house? They had to be aliens, like that movie about those scary blond twins with ESP whose families lived on top of that mountain. As an adult, Mike knew they weren't aliens, but he still didn't get it. More annoying, most of them didn't even have phones.

At least it wasn't raining. As the sun began to set, Mike chatted on the porch of a two story farmhouse with an elderly woman. A barefoot toddler of indeterminate gender played with a kitten at the old woman's feet. "We'll keep an eye out for the girl, ja," the old woman said. "But don't bother with giving me that telephone number. You'll want to go to Annie's for the closest one of those." She waved vaguely down the road.

"Thank you, ma'am," Mike said. His own grandmother had ingrained politeness into him by dint of the carrot-cake and rod, so it was automatic for Mike to ask, "Is there anything I can do for you, ma'am?"

The old woman grinned, her mouth a checkerboard of missing teeth and said, "No need, son. My children take right good care of me, ja. Even the little one." She lowered a wrinkled hand to ruffle the hair of the toddler beneath her.

When Mike got back to the stolen car, he sat in the passenger's seat and leaned the chair back. His head was killing him and his legs still ached from last night's run.

D said, "Sun's going down. Think we should try for a couple more?"

"I think we should take the car and drive west until we can steal another one," Mike said. "Let's go to Dakota. Man can lose himself in the Dakotas."

"I'm not leaving Sandy," D said. "I'm pretty sure she's pregnant."

"Did she tell you that?"

"No, but she's puking in the morning and eating pickles dipped in peanut butter in the middle of the night. It's either a baby or menopause."

"Hmmm..." Mike was inclined towards leaving D, but he didn't have any idea how to hot wire a car, and Carl had left them $30.42 for groceries, which split in half and combined with the money in Mike's account, might get him a Greyhound to Ohio. Might.

Mike was massaging the heel of his palms against his closed eyes when his pocket began to vibrate and sing.

"Someone's calling!" D exclaimed.

"Yes." Mike said, taking the phone from his pocket. As he listened to the voice on the other end, he realized with the first vestiges of hope he'd held since Carl's accident that things might be looking up. "Yes, ma'am," he repeated, incredulous at his changing luck.

Sofia had lost her memories!

When Mike had been in high school and played a decent game of football, he'd dated a red-haired nerd named Norma Jay. A week before she left him for a skinny Goth kid who wrote poems about tombstones, she'd gone on a rant once about amnesia, and how that sort of thing only happened in movies. As the Amish woman explained the situation, Mike couldn't help but grin. Amnesia! Had it been the stress, D whacking her with the bat, or the fall? Didn't matter. All that meant was he could walk right up and take her away, no one the wiser.

Mike asked again about the address, and after jotting it down on the back of a used hamburger wrapper said his goodbyes. "Take that Norma Jay," Mike said, gleefully as he flipped the phone shut.

"Who's Norma Jay?" D asked.

"Doesn't matter. We're in luck. Our Sofia's lost her memories. She's at this address," Mike handed the hamburger wrapper over to D.

"Amnesia? Isn't that like a one in a million?"

"I don't know. That's what the Amish woman," What was her name? "Annie said. Sofia didn't even know her own name."

"Are you sure this isn't a setup? Like a sting operation? The cops don't have to tell you the truth when they're trying to get you to incriminate yourself."

"Sofia wasn't even there when we visited. I doubt the cops or the Amish are that savvy to set up a sting operation in, what is it?" Mike glanced at the time on the burner phone. "Three hours."

D rubbed his hand over his thinning hair. "Yeah, you're right."

"Now let's get over there before she gets her memories back." Happy for the first time since he'd taken this godforsaken job, Mike puckered his lips and gave off a cheerful whistle.

"Zipidee do dah?" D said, the corners of his mouth turning upwards in a nervous smile.

Mike clapped his coworker on the shoulder hard enough to make D wince. "My, oh my, what a wonderful day!" he said. "A wonderful day!"

Losing the girl again did put some damper on his mood, but Mike had been lied to enough in his life to recognize the signs. The Amish man, Ah-brahm or something like that, with his unruly beard and too steady gaze, knew where the girl had gone. No matter how religious a man wanted to be, he wouldn't let a girl as pretty as Sofia run off so easy. All Mike had to do was watch, wait, and follow, and the truth would be revealed.

CHAPTER 2

Sofia held Samuel's hand all the way to his mother's farm. It was dark, and the rustling of the corn, so pleasant in the daylight, seemed to whisper ominously as the night advanced. The air was chilly, and Sofia was grateful for the thickness of her borrowed, plain clothes, even as her heels rubbed against the inside of the too-big shoes. She liked the closeness of Samuel, liked how he would occasionally tell her something about his mother, or the farm cats, or the dairy which required they all be up early in the morning to hand-milk the five aging cows. When they turned down the unpaved driveway to Samuel's home, Sofia felt a bit like she knew it already.

The house was about the same size as Abram's, though instead of a cornfield there was a large, flourishing garden and a fenced in field, presumably for grazing. In the light of the rising moon, Sofia could make out the shadowy shapes of large animals, either horses or cows, standing and sitting behind the fence. Samuel walked to the fence and stuck his hand out, clicking his tongue behind his teeth. A horse whinnied and with the dull clop of hoof beats muffled by grass, came over. Samuel's face was indistinct in the darkness, but the white of his teeth was visible in the light of the moonlight. "This is Mary," Samuel said, "Put your hand out and she'll say hello."

Hesitantly, Sofia extended her hand. The horse, Mary, huffed a hot breath against Sofia's hand and then licked at it with her large, warm tongue. Sofia giggled. "Nice horse," she said, and then asked, "Do you ride her?"

Samuel laughed. "Oh no, her job's to pull the buggy. Which she mainly only does on Sundays and when my sisters go into town to buy yarn for their knitting. The rest of the time, she mainly relaxes in the field, except when we need her to pull the plow."

"Sounds like a good life."

"Ja." Samuel sounded wistful, then he said, "Come on, my mamm will be very happy to meet you."

Sofia wondered at that, how happy Samuel's mother would be to see him bringing some strange, non-Amish person to sleep in her home. Still, she was grateful, beyond grateful. The thought of Officer Michael, no, his name was Mike, either imagination or memory offered, finding her and shooting her as it had sounded in her dream, terrified Sofia. She just wished she had something to offer in return for this gift of safety.

Though it had to be past nine-o-clock, the door was open and there was the sound of metal and sloshing water inside, as well as cheerful voices talking. Samuel shouted, "Mamm, I'm home and I have a guest."

"Samuel!" An older woman's voice sounded from inside the house. There was a loud clank, like a pot hitting the counter, and then, "What is this, bringing a guest at this hour?"

"It was an emergency, mamm. Sofia has nowhere else to stay." Samuel beckoned Sofia inside. He whispered, "Don't worry, she'll love you."

Sofia felt even more like she was intruding. She wished she could have gone back to Abram's. He had plenty of space to house a guest, and though he seemed mired in a very personal grief, in their brief time together Sofia had never felt like she was intruding. She kept herself a step behind Samuel, her hands clasped awkwardly one atop the other at her belly.

Samuel's mother came out of the kitchen, her hands on her hips. She was a short, stocky woman with visible muscles on her forearms and a square, honest face with crow's feet around her eyes and lips. She had her hair braided in the Amish style, though the braids had loosened, leaving wispy waves around her face. She looked Sofia up and down, her eyes narrowed. "Sofia's an Englischer name, isn't it?"

"She is an Englischer, mamm. Abram lent her some of his wife's clothes. She's running from something, but she's lost her memories so she doesn't know what."

"Sounds like an Englischer problem," Samuel's mother said, folding her arms over her chest and drawing herself to her full, albeit diminutive height.

"I'm very sorry," Sofia said. "I shouldn't be imposing on you like this. I can go." Where, she had no idea, but she'd slept outside once, in the rain, and this time she had warm clothes at least. Maybe she could find her way back to the shed where Samuel had stored his car.

"Out into the night by yourself?" Samuel's mother shook her head, waving a hand in front of her face to emphasize her disagreement with the idea. "I wouldn't send a friend of my son's off into the dark on her own. That's not in the sense of Christian charity."

"Are you sure?" Sofia asked. Her throat felt full and sore, and she blinked, rapidly, realizing that she might just cry.

"Oh my," Samuel's mother's expression softened, and she shook her head again, grabbing her apron in both hands and twisting it. "No, of course you will stay here. I'm Esther, though you're welcome to call me Mamm. All the kids and their friends do. They're forever bringing over friends and friends of friends, by the grace of the Good Lord. Now, Samuel, shut that door." She waved at the open door behind Sofia. "You'll let in the moths and mosquitoes, heaven help us. I'll have to put you in with Judith, that's Abram's next youngest sister. Also on rumspringa, but she's too much of us to really consider living in the Englischer world." At that, she glanced at Samuel, and her lips pursed slightly. "I believe Judith will want to be baptized soon, she's just looking to see if Aaron is going to court her seriously. Now, this way, Sofia."

Sofia followed Esther deeper into the house. Like Annie's house, the kitchen was to the left of a dining area which they passed through. There were two girls in the kitchen. One appeared to be scrubbing out a giant pot while the other took a glass container and placed tinfoil over the top. Sofia smiled at them as she passed, but only one of the girl's saw. The girl looked to be about twelve with dark hair like Samuel's pulled into two braids that fell to the small of her back. Her eyes widened as she caught sight of Sofia, but she smiled back.

Esther led Sofia up a flight of stairs and one door down a hallway into a bedroom. There were two beds in the room. No pictures hung on the walls, though above the second bed was a square of what appeared to be a quilt, patterned in geometric shapes. That bed had a pillow and another full-quilt in green with touches of yellow. The other bed had no sheets or blankets yet. Esther turned to Sofia and said, "We'll have you sleep here tonight, ja. You have no nightclothes, do you?"

"No, ma'am," Sofia said.

Esther laughed, the expression turning the somewhat forbidding planes of her face into something warm and familiar. Perhaps Sofia's mother had been similar. Sofia desperately tried to pull a memory of her, but nothing came. "It's mamm," Esther said, stressing the pronunciation. "Though I suppose I've gone old enough for both, ja."

Sofia shook her head, but Esther just laughed again. "After birthing five children and losing my husband, there's no way the good Lord would have me look like a young filly just waiting to burst out of the gate. Time paints its marks on all of us, and that's as it should be. No use in complaining." She pointed to the empty bed. "This will be yours. I'll get you some extra bedding from the closet, and you'll need something to sleep in. Can't be messing up the sheets with those soiled clothes, so you'll have to borrow something of Judith's. Luckily you're about about the same size."

"Are you sure that's okay?"

"The Ordnung says we should offer succor to our neighbor, should he be in need. And Samuel's a good lad, if confused. He wouldn't have brought you here without need."

At that moment, Sofia's stomach growled.

"You're starving, child! Why didn't Samuel tell me we needed to feed you? My daughters and I are just finishing up with the washing, but we'll have some leftovers for you, if you don't mind it cold."

"That would be lovely, thank you," Sofia said. Tears threatened to fall again. Here she was, a complete stranger, and these people continually opened their hearts and homes to her. It felt strange and wonderful at the same time. Sofia wondered if her own people were like that. Considering her dreams and what had happened to her, she doubted it. If her family had been so warm, so welcoming, would Sofia have forgotten them so easily? It seemed uncharitable to think of them in that way, though. Who knew why she'd lost her memories of her own life?

Sofia followed Esther back to the kitchen, where Samuel was laughing and joking with the two other girls. Esther strode out ahead of Sofia, and her index finger extended, jammed it into Samuel's chest. "Why didn't you tell me this poor girl was starving?"

Samuel had the grace to look contrite, his sharp cheekbones flushing pink. "I'm sorry, mamm. I think you just took her away so quickly, not that it's anyone's fault but mine."

"Well, see to her getting something now. And you as well. You'll both have to eat cold chicken and last Sunday's bread."

"Yes, mamm."

Sofia noted that Samuel's pronunciation was indistinguishable from the "ma'am" that Esther had corrected her about earlier. Samuel took out a plate of carved chicken and butter, while the other girl grabbed two plates from the cupboards and silverware from the drawer beneath it. A loaf of bread was placed on the table too. Though Esther had disparaged its quality, the bread and meat looked positively mouthwatering to Sofia. Upon seeing the food, her hands began to shake. Or maybe they had been shaking before but she just hadn't noticed.

At Esther's prompting, Sofia took a chicken leg and a large hunk of bread. Esther slathered the bread in butter as Sofia stood at the counter with her plate until Esther pushed her gently into the dining room. In the center of the large table, a gas lantern was visible from the lantern-light in the kitchen. Samuel took it and lit it with expert practice. The light was weaker than Sofia was used to and lent and ethereal quality to the table and the plates atop it.

After they sat, Samuel closed his eyes and clasped his hands, "Dear God, thank you for the food we are about to receive for the nourishment of our bodies, and thank you for giving me the chance to help a fellow person in need. Please allow us to use these gifts of your bounty for your service, in the Lord's name, amen."

"Amen," Sofia repeated. Again, she was amazed by the quiet faith of Samuel's words. He opened his eyes and taking up a fork began to tuck into the meat and bread in front of him. Sofia did the same, and for a time there was only the sound of the girls chatting in the other room, the slosh of water and scrape of sponge on metal, as they washed, and the softer tap of silverware on china. The bread, though a bit hard on the outside was soft on the inside, and the butter seemed richer than anything her taste buds could have imagined. The chicken also seemed to melt on her tongue, its spices subtle but well used. Soon Sofia was licking her fingers clean. She was tempted to run her thumb along the bottom of the bowl to get the juices, but that seemed impolite. Instead, she took sips at the lemonade. The coolness of the glass comforted her as much as the sweetness of the beverage.

As she ate, the fear that had shadowed her seemed to fade. The lantern-light was steady, and it cast a pleasant orange glow about the table. Samuel was chewing on his last bite when Sofia put her fork down, spokes against the plate. "That was delicious," Sofia said.

"My mamm is one of the best cooks in our district."

"Now don't be giving me airs, ja," Esther shouted from the kitchen.

"Of course not, mamm," Samuel said, and then leaning towards Sofia, the lantern-light setting a mischievous twinkle to his eyes, added in a whisper, "She is though. Everyone asks after her recipes."

Sofia felt a warmth in her stomach, more than the food, at Samuel's simple and direct praise of his mother's abilities. There was love in this house, a light of caring where Abram's home had contained need, sadness and bitter want.

"What puts your thoughts so far away?" Samuel asked.

"I just wonder if my own home is as filled with love like yours," Sofia said. It wasn't a lie, she realized as she spoke. The need to know where she came from, who she had been, was sharp like a knife pushing out from inside her chest.

"Your family must be looking for you. Have you tried to contact them?"

"I tried, at Annie's," Sofia said, letting her gaze rest on Samuel in hopes that he would leave it at that. There was no reason to have Samuel's mother become even more embroiled in Sofia's problems.

"That's good them. I suppose our Samuel charmed you into coming with him." Esther smacked her tongue as though she had tasted something bitter. "He's always been good with your Englischer ways."

Sofia stared down at her plate, pushing at the remains of her chicken bone with her fork. "Samuel has been very kind."

Esther stood. "I'll see to your bedding," she said, and walked away from the table towards the back of the house.

"And to have given us someone as kind as you, Sofia, I'm sure you must have come from love." Samuel said the words earnestly. Though he had barely known her, he saw her as something beautiful, not for her body, but for some portion of spirit maybe, because she had listened and tried to understand. "I don't know what those policemen might have intended, but I'm glad that you are safe, and that I was able to help."

"Thank you," Sofia said again. It seemed she was always having to thank people. One day soon, she hoped, she would be able to give these people something in return for their kindness. The exhaustion of the day had caught up with Sofia and she yawned deeply, hiding it behind her hand. Every part of her felt heavy. Her legs, her eyelids, her jaw even. The food, the contentment of it, now made her want to rest. She yawned again. Her body hurt, the bruises on her arms and legs and the dull throb in her head. Her feet were scratched and bruised, and above her heels the skin had been rubbed raw from the too large shoes.

"You look tired," Samuel said, and then shouted, "Mamm, I think we should take Sofia to bed. She's falling into her lemonade."

"I sent Miri up with it and her clothes for the night," Esther shouted back. Measured footfalls sounded over the hardwood floors. Esther stepped in and said, "Samuel, clear the plates. Now, Miss Sofia, you come up with me, ja."

"Yes, mamm," Sofia said, careful to get the pronunciation right. She followed Esther again up the stairs and down the hallway to the second door. The bedding had been made, and a long nightdress was draped over the quilt that covered the bed. It was yellow and blue, mostly, with patches of red and green. The nightdress was plain, like the clothing she wore, but when Sofia touched the fabric, it was soft and cool.

"This should do you for now. Judith may or may not come in tonight. She certainly is enjoying the recreational side of your Englischer world. But as I always say, she's welcome here and welcome to come back. That's our way. Though to be honest, if anyone's to be leaving, it'll be Samuel. He's even got his own place, though he shares it with three other guys and sleeps here most nights."

"I think..." Was it her place to say anything? She was an uninvited guest in Samuel's home, and already her presence had brought violence, not only from the men who were hunting her, but also in Samuel bringing the gun into their home. At the same time, it had been obvious from Sofia and Samuel's earlier conversation that he was feeling pulled in two directions and that it was making him very upset. And his mother now, with her honest, open face also mirrored the same concerns. Sofia wanted to help, to do something to right the scales of debt between them, and maybe their God had put her in their lives to show what she'd seen. Sofia took a breath, and letting her fingers brush along the stitching of the quilt over her borrowed bed, asked, "Would you be terribly angry if he chose to leave?"

"Angry?" Esther's brows lowered in confusion. "Where would you get that idea?"

"He seems very concerned about letting you down, and the memory of his father."

Esther fingers tightened around the pillow she was holding. She stood ramrod straight, her gaze faraway. "Samuel's father was a good man, and he taught Samuel to be a good man, a Godly man. But a man's faith and how he chooses to follow it is his own decision. I would never take that from him, as much as I might want him to choose my path. I love my son, and I love my God too much for that foolishness."

Sofia took a step towards Esther. She was so impressed with this strong, compassionate woman. "Have you told him this?"

"Of course. But Samuel carries his own guilt about the accident. I think it's keeping him from knowing what he truly wants." And with that Esther placed the pillow at the head of the bed, and after fluffing it with maybe a bit more force than needed, said, "I'll take Rebekah's dress. It'll need to go in with the washing tomorrow. You're lucky you came in on a Friday and not Sunday, otherwise you'd have to wait a week for the washing. Not that you'd be here so long, I suspect."

"You'll want to do your washing up in the bathroom down the hall. I've left you a washcloth and toothbrush with Judith's nightdress." She strode past Sofia towards the entrance, pausing at a gas lantern that was lit and hung on a hook beside the door. "You'll need to take this down the hall and into the bathroom as it's too dark to see now. Just turn this when you're ready to go to sleep," Esther demonstrated the mechanism, dimming the lamp even further before adding more gas to make the lantern-light flame more brightly again. "I can't say I'm glad Samuel brought you, Miss Sofia. It's nothing against you. You seem like a woman who is carrying her own burdens, and that is between you and our Lord. You're a good person and there's a light in you that's there for anyone to see. It's only that a pretty girl is like to muddle a man's mind more than any convenience of the Englischer world. So please, by the Lord's name, be careful of my son's heart, and your own."

With that, Esther shut the door, leaving Sofia alone with her thoughts. She wanted, so badly, the confidence of faith that everyone around her seemed so easily to take for granted. She laid backwards diagonally atop the quilt, her head brushing the wall and her legs bent over the opposite edge.

Esther was right, she couldn't continue like this, caught between fear and complacency and living at the charity of strangers. As Samuel had said, on Monday, she would go into the town proper and try to find out who she was and how to contact her own people. Or maybe she would call the Philadelphia police, if the Lancaster police were compromised. She'd have to use a different phone. Annie's house, as warm and welcoming as it had been, was no longer safe.

Sofia took the lantern in her right hand with the nightdress and washcloth hung over her left arm and tiptoed down the hallway to the bathroom. Placing the lantern on a hook above and to the right of the sink, Sofia stripped herself of Rebekah's clothes, her fingers working awkwardly over the clasps. She felt with each layer she was losing a bit of the person she had begun to build. She took the bar of soap at the edge of the sink, and turning on the water and dropping in the plug for the drain, briskly cat-washed herself. The water was lukewarm at best, but refreshing enough, and Sofia liked the feeling of clean. She also unbraided her hair; the tightness of Samuel's braids had begun to make her head hurt, and then she brushed her teeth.

Like Abram's bathroom, there was only a tiny mirror mounted above the sink, just enough for her to see the reflection of her mouth in the glass to make sure there wasn't anything left in her teeth. Sofia stepped back from the mirror, in order to get a better view of her face, but she could only see herself in sections: her nose and the dip where it met her forehead, her right cheek, her left eye. The lantern light was too dim for her to make a fair assessment of herself anyhow. Even if she'd had all of her memories, she might not have recognized herself, draped in a long cotton nightdress and her hair falling in a loose knot from the nape of her neck.

"Dear God," Sofia prayed, the whisper coming to her lips awkwardly, like an old joint worked by an atrophied muscle, all creaking to life. "Thank you for bringing me to here, to all who have helped me. Thank you for keeping me safe."

She closed her eyes, and though she heard no voice, through the open window, the gentle movements of the breeze through the fields seemed an answer, an expression of love.

CHAPTER 3

The smartest thing Abram could do, he knew, was not to go tearing out in the middle of the night on his buggy to try and find out where Samuel had taken Sofia. Though there were only two options really: (1) wherever Samuel kept his Englischer apartment or, (2) at his mother's house. The latter was the most likely. So as he stayed while the young men and women finished their singing circle, a strange nervousness settled in his belly, not, if he was honest with himself, out of fear for Sofia's safety, but out of a vague fear for her virtue, alone with Samuel in the dark. Unlike Abram, Samuel had not taken his vows nor chosen as yet to follow the Ordnung. Abram knew from his time in the band that the dictates of propriety that organized Amish life were not the same for Englischers. A man and woman could do as they liked without promises.

Abram asked to help the women finish with the dishes, though it wasn't his place. He simply couldn't stand to be idle. Eventually Annie sent him out back with a lantern and a stack of wood for chopping. Abram went at it with vigor, but the agitation didn't dissipate even as his limbs became sore and leaden.

What did it matter to Abram how the Englischer and Samuel passed their time? Abram had no stake beyond Christian charity in the future of this particular Englischer woman. Yes, he had promised his God that he would open his heart to the possibility of love, but that meant that he would find a good, virtuous Amish woman and share the life with her that he had wanted with Rebekah: a home, work, and many children to bring light and life to the walls of his empty home. He certainly wasn't going to turn aside from his promise to serve his God or his community.

Annie led him to the spare bedroom. There was one other young man already asleep in the bed by the window. Annie whispered, "That's the friend Samuel brought and left when he ran off with the pretty Englischer girl. I swear..." but she was smiling.

Abram said, "Samuel is only helping her, because she needed aid."

Annie just looked at him, "Oh Abram." She shook her head. "Have you prayed about this?"

"For Sofia? Yes, of course." Would that Abram could have gone with her, though how he could have helped further, he couldn't really say. "God gave her to my care."

"Yes, of course," Annie said. "There's a spare toothbrush under the sink, should you need it."

With that she left, leaving Abram with the second bed as his own. Abram stripped his pants, suspenders and jacket. As always, Abram prayed before sleep. Usually his prayers were simple things, gratitude for the seasons, the sturdiness of his home, the customers who bought his furniture, but mostly gratitude that God had allowed him to bear his grief another day. Today he added another prayer that Sofia, wherever she was, would be safe and that she might find her way back to herself. He did his best not to think of it more than that.

The next morning woke cloudy and chill. The other boy had snored off and on through the night, and between that, the strange bed, and the sense of anticipation, the need to be doing something, anything, that he hadn't felt in years, Abram drifted in a state between sleeping and wakefulness that had him up with the sun, limbs heavy and head pounding. Abram put back on the clothes he'd been wearing yesterday. He'd just done up his suspenders when the boy across from him woke.

"Morning," Abram said, not really wanting to start a conversation.

The boy grinned, his hair a rat's nest of light brown hair. His teeth jutted out a bit, that in combination with his thinness giving him the appearance of a mildly emaciated squirrel. "Morning, ja," the boy said. "You're the one who brought that Englischer girl!"

"Ja."

"For a minute there, I thought she might have been your wife. How'd you meet her?"

"That really isn't my story alone to tell," Abram said. "Where are you from?" The boy was clearly Amish, and Abram could vaguely remember having seen him before, but they weren't from the same district.

"Oh, Bishop Price," the boy said. "I'm Emmanuel, but people just call me Manny." He sat up, throwing the sheet over his bare legs and extended his hands. He'd slept only in his underwear, and wisps of wiry hair dusted his chest and arms.

"Nice to meet you, Manny," Abram said, taking the other boy's hand and shaking it.

"So, why was she dressed plain if she's an Englischer? Tourist?"

"She needed clothes," Abram said, pulling the sheets back to the end of the bed and folding them for Annie's washing. He folded the quilt as well and placed it opposite the sheets, putting the bare pillow on top. "It's our duty to help those in need."

"So she isn't wanted for a crime, you don't think?"

"Why would you think that?" Abram's response was a bit sharper than the question warranted, and Manny shifted away from him, stammering, "Well, I thought with the police, and she ran and..."

"Let the man who is without sin cast the first stone," Abram said. He stood. "Excuse me."

"Wait! I'm sorry, I didn't meant to offend you."

"No offense taken, ja," Abram forced a smile. Had he ever been so young?

There were buttered rolls and fried eggs in glass containers on the kitchen counter, still piping hot. One of Annie's daughters was spooning up a plate. "Mornin' Abram," she said, handing him an empty plate. Abram took the eggs and two rolls and ate. He hardly tasted the food. It would make the most sense for him to go back to his home. He had to get his furniture to auction, and as it was he would already be late when the van came to pick him up at seven. Best to cancel for this week. He could sell the chairs next week, or send them to one of the Amish shops on consignment, though he'd make less money for the sale.

He called and canceled, ate quickly, and then harnessed Ruthie and started his buggy home. At the intersection of the dirt road that lead to Annie's home and the main road sat a station wagon. Inside were two men in police uniforms. Abram recognized the one from yesterday, Officer Maglione. He stepped out of his car as Abram's buggy approached, and walked into the road to block Ruthie's way. "Excuse me!" The man yelled. In the morning sunlight, the uniform seemed ill-fitting, the black of the jacket not quite matching that of the pants. He carried a police belt with handcuffs, a club, and a gun holstered at his hip. The gun holster seemed a bit small for the gun as well.

"Good morning officer," Abram said with a smile. "How can I help you?"

Maglione returned Abram's smile, his gaze studying Abram's face as though he wasn't sure if he recognized the man he was looking at or not. Abram suspected one Amish looked basically like the next to this man, who Abram was beginning to doubt more and more was an officer of any law.

"I'm searching for a missing girl," Maglione said. "She was recently seen in this area, and we're wondering if you have any information about her." Maglione continued with a detailed description of Sofia, ending with, "It's possible she was injured in a struggle with her abductors."

"That poor woman. This sort of thing is a travesty under God," Abram said, "And I hope that God in his infinite wisdom roots out these abominations who wear the skin of men, who chose to give such abuse to a woman, so that they might feel His judgment upon their souls for the rest of their living days and beyond. Yes, I shall pray on this." Abram spoke with conviction, pitching his voice as he did for a concert, allowing his words to flow through him and Maglione's eyes widened as he stepped back. Abram smiled. "Is there anything else I can do for you officer?"

"N...no...thank you," Maglione stuttered.

With a practiced snap of the reins, Abram urged Ruthie onwards, onto the road, her hoofs ringing against the pavement like the heartbeat of a higher power.

CHAPTER 4

When Abram arrived home, he gathered up all of Rebekah's old clothes and placed them in a bag. His heart felt lighter for doing this. Instead of a shroud that he kept hidden as a reminder of loss, these became a gift. It was what Rebekah would have wanted. He wished he'd had the courage to donate her clothes before, to shake free this layer of dust that had fallen over his life and begin again, firm in the knowledge that living was not a betrayal of all he had lost. He wasn't sure if he had the courage now, but with God's help, he would try. For Sofia's sake, if nothing else.

Next Abram loaded his buggy up again and taking care to travel a different route in case the two false policemen chose to follow, made his way to Samuel's mother's home. Unlike most of the others in the area, Samuel's family kept cows. There were only three, for milking for the family and to sell to the neighbors, still for most this was an embarrassing misuse of resources. Only the large size of their farm allowed them enough space to graze the cows comfortably and still have a sprawling vegetable garden from which to sell goods. Now, as it was nearing noon, the cows ambled in the fenced off field in front of the barn with the horse for company.

As Samuel approached the house, the women were hanging the weekly wash. Clotheslines were hung in a circular arrangement in the patch of mowed grass between the front of the house and the field. Esther's short, sturdy form was easily discernible, as was the youngest, a girl of about eight, running between her mother and her older sisters with clothespins. All of the women looked over as the buggy approached, and one waved. It took a moment to recognize that it was Sofia.

She had her hair plaited Amish style, and in the midday sun, the false blonde seemed to glisten. Abram waved back. She held a shirt between both hands, and shaking it out twice, clothes pinned it to the line by the shoulders. Then, hands freed, she said something to one of the other women before walking towards his buggy. The air was warm enough to walk barefoot, but she still wore Rebekah's shoes. She winced as the toe caught on a rock at the edge of the path that led to the house. The shoes were too big for her, and Abram wished he had something better to offer. She'd changed her clothes, a dark green dress and matching kapp that made her eyes shine green as well.

"Abram," she said, when she was close enough. She smiled, her lips a rosebud pink with straight white teeth flashing between. "Thank you, so much, for everything."

Abram averted his gaze, the admiration of hers embarrassing him. "It was nothing."

"You saved my life, I know it."

"I think you may be right, about those officers" Abram said. "They were at the entrance to the road from Annie's house. I think they were checking all the buggies, but their uniforms were wrong. The one did carry a gun though."

"He was big, wasn't he? A big man?"

"Very large," Abram agreed. "And his uniform didn't fit him properly. Even the gun wasn't properly holstered."

Her eyes widened. "Do you know a lot about guns?"

"Only what I've seen from the police around. And in Philadelphia. I spent some time there during my rumspringa."

"What did these men want?"

"You, I'm assuming. It will be better when you regain your memories."

"Yes..." her voice trailed off. "I guess."

"Of course it will be good. Don't you want to know who you are?"

"I do! And yet..." She gave a sigh, pushing her hands into the hips of her dress as though she expected there to be pockets. "There has to be a reason these men want to hurt me. What if it's something I did? There's a noise in my dream, so loud it cancels out all thought except to run. And so I ran. I can see them, but I can't see their faces. What if it's me? What if I did something so terrible that they want me to pay? And what if I deserve it?"

"You don't." Abram put Ruthie's reins aside and climbed down from the seat. When he was close enough to touch her, he stopped. It was improper to be so close to a woman who was not his wife, one he wasn't even courting. "You can't. God would not have worked through me to help you, had you deserved their actions."

Sofia blinked rapidly, and wiped the top of her hand beneath tearing eyes. "Thank you, Abram." Before he could step back, she grabbed at his waist, pressing him into a tight hug. "Thank you."

The warmth of her body felt like a homecoming, and against all his good judgment, Abram found himself leaning into the embrace. He wanted to cup her face and bring her lips up to his. He hadn't felt this sort of desire for a woman since his wife had died, and it both frightened and compelled him.

"Abram! Sofia!" Esther's voice shouted from the field.

Flustered, Abram stepped back. "I'm sorry, I mean, we shouldn't do that." He tugged at his jacket unnecessarily. Had Sofia felt the same heat between them? How could he allow himself such lustful thoughts for a woman who had only made a simple gesture of friendship and gratitude? He couldn't meet her gaze.

My God, Abram prayed, desperate to exorcise these wrongful thoughts from his being, *please save me from myself.*

"Are you okay?," Sofia asked. Esther was crossing the field towards them, her usually cheerful face a mask, only the tightness of her lips and shoulders giving away any emotion at all.

"Ja," Abram said, turning back to the buggy. "I have some clothes for you to use, for as long as you need them." And would he be able to bear seeing her in Rebekah's clothes now, knowing as he did that he wanted her? It would be better if he left, immediately. The weight of his desire was so much that he sought excuses to weigh against his better judgment. He should have gone to the auction and sold his wares. He should have gone to the bishop for guidance. He should have gone anywhere but here.

"Oh, Abram," Sofia asked, placing a hand on his shoulder. She did it so lightly, the touch was more a whisper of breeze than the actual weight of a human hand. Abram closed his eyes for a few seconds, letting the smell of manure and fresh earth fill his nose.

At that moment, the door to the farmhouse opened, and from it Samuel yelled, "Abram!" He smiled, fanning his face with the brim of his hat, but his grin was a touch too wide and after the briefest glance at Sofia and Abram, Samuel started at an-almost run towards the buggy. One of Samuel's younger brothers shadowed him, dashing to keep up with Samuel's large strides.

When Samuel got close enough, Abram explained, "Just delivering some clothes for Sofia. Please be careful. The two false policemen from yesterday are still looking for Sofia. Don't let them know she's here."

"Are you sure they're fakes?"

"Their uniforms didn't fit correctly, and the one tried to threaten me."

Waving, Esther stepped from the field onto the path. "Oy!" she yelled. "Abram, what are you doing here?"

"Abram found Sofia," Samuel explained. "He brought her to the singing circle."

"Excuse me, ma'am," Abram said. "I didn't mean to impose. Sofia here was lost in these trees here around the farms, and I thought she might need help. Then I found out she didn't know anything about herself, so we took her to Annie's to use the phone. A pair of police officers had come by earlier and left their numbers, claiming that they were looking for her, but Sofia heard one of their voices and it scared her, terribly. Samuel said he'd take her away somewhere safe, and I think that's a good thing because I saw that same officer this morning, and I don't believe he's with the police at all."

"And you didn't go to Annie's and use her phone to tell the real police all of this!" Esther gave Samuel and Abram a firm punch in the arm. Samuel winced. "Shame on you," Esther said. "This girl's family must be worried sick about her, and here you have her at my farm playing tourist!"

"She doesn't know anything about herself," Abram said, hoping to diffuse Esther's growing ire, but Esther was hearing none of it, her wide, honest face becoming more and more animated as she walked towards him, her index finger extended like a fire-poker. "I can understand such nonsense from Samuel, but you, a grown man..."

"It's not his fault," Sofia cut in. "When I heard that man, I knew he was dangerous. I think he was one of the men who kidnapped me, though I never saw their faces." As soon as she said the words, her expression froze, and a hiss of breath ran through her teeth. "I remember. There were two men, one stocky and the other skinny and they wore stockings so I never saw their faces. One hit me with a bat," she touched her temple, "and the other tried to shoot me when I ran. But I got away from them."

Esther asked, "Are you sure the two men dressed as Englischer police are the same two men that hurt you?" she kept her voice low and calm as though trying to tame a frightened animal.

Sofia opened her mouth, then closed it. She was breathing shallowly, and she pulled at one of her braids. "Maybe, I don't know. The voice seemed familiar but..."

"We'll need to report this to the Lancaster authorities," Esther said. "If there are two criminals running around here pretending to be police, they will need to be informed. Abram, take Sofia and Samuel in your buggy and go to Annie's again to use her phone. They'll need to hear it from Sofia as she's the one who was attacked."

"I can't go back to Annie's," Sofia said, her voice taking on the high pitch of approaching hysteria. "They're watching Annie's. And they have guns."

Abram nodded. "They are armed. I saw that this morning. I can't take Sofia knowingly into danger. I won't."

Sofia took a step towards Abram, as though she was shielding herself in his larger shadow. Abram was moved by the show of trust. The insane, fanciful part of himself wanted to put his arm around her, to have the right to hold her as a man held a woman, which seemed not only a betrayal of Rebekah but also of himself. She was only beginning to gain back her memories, and those memories were of fear and pain. Of course she would find comfort in the safety and community that the Amish offered. But when she returned to herself, she would also return to her own community. Her own passions. A woman as tough, beautiful, and kind as Sofia would certainly have many suitors at home. It would be a wonder if she wasn't already married, though at least she wore no ring, nor did her ring finger show the indentation that came from wearing such a ring for a long period of time. Not that he should have paid these details such mind.

"Perhaps if we just tell the police that there are two officers who are acting suspiciously, and give the name of the one. Maglione?" Abram suggested. "We don't have to talk about Sofia at all. Englischer police should be concerned about pretenders no matter what, ja?"

"That's an excellent idea," Samuel said. "And Sofia and I were going to go to into town on Monday and try and use the library's computers to try and see if we could find out more about her. We should be able to talk to the police there also."

"Unless these two men are real police," Sofia said. "If they are, then what?"

"We'll leave that in the hands of the Almighty," Esther said. "Our Lord certainly won't allow you to come to further harm. In the meantime, let's have Abram go down to Annie's and make that call today."

"And you'll come back, right, after you're done and tell us how it went?" Sofia asked, her hazel eyes shining as she looked up into his. "Please."

Esther said, "He'll be here for church tomorrow, and he can tell you then." She pointed at Ruthie and said sharply, "There's no point in working his poor horse to exhaustion."

"Oh! Right, of course. I hadn't thought. Poor Ruthie! Will she be okay?"

"She's a strong girl," Abram said, his face warming again. Why should he be so happy that Sofia remembered the name of his horse? "I'll just be passing along these clothes before I go."

"Well, it's decided then," Esther said. "Sofia, go back to hanging the wash with the girls, and Samuel, you have work in the fields. I'll take the clothing from you and put it in Judith's room for the time being." Esther waved her hand, shooing the other two away. Abram didn't dare steal a glance back at Sofia. It did him no good to entertain that futile hope that she might still be looking to him for comfort or something more. Instead, he walked to the buggy and took the bundle of Rebekah's clothing from the seat. He'd held them together with a long piece of with string, crossed at the bottom, wrapped around each side, and tied at the top in a bow.

Esther, who took the clothes, thanked him and then continued in Pennsylvania Dutch, "You had best be careful."

"I have no intention of confronting these men," Abram said. Well, he had no intention of doing so again at least. "But neither should they be running loose in our community."

Esther's lips pursed and the wrinkles between her brows deepened as she huffed through her nose. "I know you aren't that kind of fool, Abram. I mean be careful of the girl. You want to court her."

"I wouldn't dream..."

"I wasn't talking about your dreams. You're a man and too long alone, and this Englischer girl is pretty, and kind, and she needs help, and don't think we all can't see how you blame yourself for what happened to Rebekah." Esther closed her eyes, her shoulders slumping. "You like her, and this Sofia seems fond of you as well, as fond as one can be for the short time you've known each other. But Sofia can't give herself to you, not as she is, even if she wants to. And you can't use her to atone for your wife's mistakes."

It was as though Esther's words had torn all of the breath from Abram's lungs. He was fond of Sofia. There was no point in lying to himself further about that, not when it was so obvious that Esther noticed it within a few minutes of seeing Sofia and Abram together. And it was stupid to believe that Sofia could promise him anything, certainly not before she knew who she was and what she actually wanted. But he had never thought that this desire to protect her had less to do with virtue and more with the base usage of another individual to exonerate himself of his own sins.

"Dear God..." Abram breathed. He reached for the bundle of clothes. Now the gift of them seemed an abomination as severe as he'd accused the men who had attacked Sofia, whether it had been the false police or others, of committing. "She shouldn't wear these," Abram said.

"No, she shouldn't," Esther agreed, stepping out of Abram's reach. "Sofia can wear Judith's clothes, heaven knows Judith isn't using them right now. And we'll offer these at Church tomorrow to any who have need."

"Yes, of course. You're right." Abram touched his beard, then his collarbone, before settling his hands at his sides. "Yes. That's for the best."

Esther maneuvered the clothes into her left arm and then took Abram's right hand. "You're a good man, Abram. Your wife made her decisions and so did you, but that's all in the past. Only the good Lord has the right to judge us for our mistakes. Let Him forgive you, so that you can forgive yourself."

"Thank you," Abram said. His eyes stung, and there was a lump inside his throat. He hadn't cried since the afternoon Rebekah had died, the final scream still echoing in his dreams as she'd squeezed his hand tight enough to crush his bones together, and then loosening as the midwife tried desperately to get the pale, bloody bundle that would have been his and Rebekah's son to breathe. She'd have made it in an Englischer hospital, with their needles, bags of blood and endlessly beeping machines. If he'd insisted on taking her, Rebekah would have lived. Abram turned back to the buggy, leaning inside as though searching for something but actually using the sheltering darkness as a compress to keep the tears at bay. Abram breathed, wiping one hand beneath each eye to rub his tears away. To erase them, as he'd striven these three years to erase the awful sound of his wife's final, agonizing goodbye.

When Abram had pulled himself together again, he leaned back from the buggy, pulling the door shut. He'd need water for Ruthie before forcing her to pull this buggy again through the heat. He walked into the garden, his feet sweating in his boots as he tramped past ripe tomatoes and cucumbers, before catching sight of one of the younger boys. "Can you give me a bucket," Abram asked. "And do you have outside water?"

The boy lead Abram to both, and Abram returned, placing the full bucket under Ruthie's muzzle. The horse drank deeply, draining the bucket almost to the bottom. Abram patted her side, and after returning the bucket to the boy, alighted into the buggy and turned it back toward Annie's home. His thoughts were troubled by Esther's words for the entire ride.

CHAPTER 5

As Sofia walked back towards the clotheslines, grass tickling at her ankles even through her socks, the memory of Abram's touch lingered in Sofia's flesh. She didn't dare look back. Though she'd only known Abram a short time, there was a connection between them. She hadn't even thought when she'd forced him into an embrace, and after a moment, the tension in his muscles had eased as his arms tightened around her. Their bodies fit. She'd wanted to tilt her head up and see if he might kiss her. There was a fire in him, dampened by grief, and like banked coals needing simply air and movement to be brought back to brilliant life.

But what if what she felt was simply infatuation? She was a child in a woman's body; her knowledge was a muscle memory of facts and habits, but with only the faintest hint of memories to give her an understanding of her own dimensions.

"Sofia!" Mary ran towards the road. Her kapp had come loose again, dropping to the nape of her neck and she stopped just short of crashing into Sofia, shoving the kapp up and tied the string under her chin in a hurried bow before throwing her arms around Sofia's waist. Mary looked up, her chin digging into Sofia's stomach and grinned with her missing canine. "You're not going with him, are you? You're going to stay for the cleaning right?" she asked for about the twentieth time. "We have to get the living room ready for church tomorrow!"

"Yes, I'm here until Monday at least, provided your mother lets me stay." After the girl unwrapped her arms from Sofia's waist, Sofia took Mary's hand and they walked together towards Judith and her younger sister Miriam, a ruddy faced girl who looked about twelve.

Mary rattled on in the same vein she'd been going along all morning, "Oh, mamm is so happy that Samuel brought a woman home, though it'd be better if you were Amish. Are you going to join us when you get your memories back? You're not so good at washing, but you'll get better. And if you stay, then you and Samuel can build a house on the east side of the cornfields and we can visit you anytime we want."

The child's simple delight at the idea was enchanting, but there was something about the tightness around her eyes and the way she kept stealing glances up, as though Sofia was something both attractive and dangerous that made Sofia feel like a thief. Or a potential thief. It was clear that Mary adored her older brother, and now Sofia, a stranger, had come with the power to take Samuel away. No, he wouldn't be exiled from his home simply for choosing a different path, but he also wouldn't be able to live here. He'd have his own life outside of their community with new experiences he couldn't share.

Sofia couldn't imagine how difficult it would be to be forced to make such a choice.

Though Samuel had already chosen to challenge his future when he'd bought the gun, at least she'd had tried to keep him from bringing it here. She didn't want him to lose everything trying to help her. Then she really would become a thief. Sofia hung the clothes, chattering with the two older girls first about the weather and their work, and for Miriam about the last year of school and how difficult it would be to see her friends afterward with all of the work she had to do on the farm.

"It's not so bad," the oldest said. "And you have plenty of time for reading, though maybe not those novels you favor."

"I want to go to France," Miriam said. "I want to see the Arc de Triomphe." She pronounced it in the English way, 'try-umph" and Sofia corrected her before she even knew she had done so.

"Tree-umph," the preteen grinned, her face reddening a hint further. "French sounds odd."

They finished the clothes in that way, talking about their lives, their neighbors, friends and dreams. Sofia was mostly quiet, soaking in the conversation as a balm against her troubled thoughts. The rooster had woken Sofia before dawn, screaming off and on through sunrise and into their breakfast of eggs and bread. She'd enjoyed the camaraderie as she and the family tackled the flurry of activities necessary to prepare the house for tomorrow's church service. Together they had washed the tablecloths and everyone's clothing, hand-scrubbing the clothing while running the tablecloths through the wash and spinning them dry again using a hand-cranked machine that looked like it had been used for this purpose for the past hundred years at least. Sofia had been pronounced hopeless at the scrubbing, her technique too firm for the delicates and too hesitant for deep set stains.

The men and boys had occupied themselves with checking the stools and benches for signs of disrepair, and mending in general, as well as maintaining the fields, hen-house, and dairy.

"You girls stay clear of that rooster, ja," Samuel had warned them when Sofia ventured too close to the fenced off area that was the rooster's exclusive domain. "He's a small beast, but he'll take a chunk out of you for sure. As good as a guard dog, those roosters is, except they see everything and everyone as their enemy."

Mary had rolled her eyes behind her big-brother's back, and once he was gone whispered, "Samuel's the only one of us dumb enough to try and play with that stupid, cranky thing. He's still got a scar on his ankle where it bit him, and he broke his arm trying to get away, but Judith says he got a cast, from an Englischer hospital!" she declared the last as though it was both a privilege and badge of honor.

At the end of the day came the cooking. "Everyone'll bring a dish for after the service," Esther explained, so we're really only needing to prepare dinner tonight. The men will have a smoke outside most likely. We'll all need to take our baths, and we want to be early to bed, so we're up in enough time to greet the Bishop."

Everyone agreed, and after dinner, Sofia followed Judith up to the bedroom. Esther came soon after, and after rifling through the bottom of Judith's drawers, pulled out a white shirt, and navy blue dress with matching kapp. "These'll fit you better than what Abram gave you," she said gruffly. "You just fold these up and leave them on the dresser after your shower, and I'll be giving them back to him. No fair to either of you, him putting you in Rebekah's clothes, though from what he said there was a right, immediate need, ja."

Sofia nodded. She certainly didn't want to impose on Abram or the memory of his wife. "Of course," she said. "I'd always intended to return them."

"Never thought any different, child. Now, my Judith doesn't mind if you borrow her nightdress again."

"No mamm," Judith said, unbraiding the first of her tight plaits. "You're welcome to whatever you like."

"Thank you," Sofia said. Her throat felt thick with gratitude. She wished again she had some way to pay these people back for their kindness.

When Esther had left, Judith asked, "So, is there anything between you and Abram?"

"Nothing," Sofia said, too quickly.

Judith raised her eyebrows. "Nothing! Sounds like something to me, ja."

"It's only, he was the first to help me, when I came to his farm," Sofia explained the entire story again. It seemed remarkable that such dramatic things had happened to her, were still happening to her.

When she had finished, Judith asked, "So you don't remember anything? Even now?"

"I think..." Sofia sighed. "I don't know. I had a dream last night about a beautiful home and dancing." She wouldn't mention the man. The thought of him made her feel uncomfortable, as though she was being unfaithful, but was it loyalty to this dream or to Abram, or even to Samuel? It had seemed as though they lived together, or at least that she was comfortable enough in his home to change for a party. His home, not hers. That truth settled through her body. She said, "I think I might have been rich. Maybe that's why those two men wanted me, to get money."

"That's so awful!" Judith crossed the room from her own bed to sit beside Sofia and place an arm around her shoulder. "Do you remember any of your family or friends?"

"Nothing," Sofia said. More than the confusion of this dream man, it was the lack of any family presence that made Sofia feel that her previous life might have been colder than anything she could imagine. Didn't she have a mother, someone warm and decisive like Esther, who kept all of her children in line through a mix of firm guidance and love? "I remember running, and someone trying to grab me, and a gunshot." "A gunshot?" the horror in Judith's voice made the question an accusation. She squeezed Sofia tighter. "There is no excuse for anyone to threaten another human life, especially with a tool made only for killing. I can't even imagine anyone in my life daring God's will to touch such a thing."

In addition to sadness and frustration, now came a crushing guilt. It was only because of Sofia that Samuel had been compelled to bring the gun from the safekeeping of his shed into this warm and loving home. It would break Sofia's heart to see Samuel hold this thing, to point it at another with the thought of using it, in the presence of his family, who would certainly condemn him for such a step, no matter how good intentioned. She had to convince Samuel to throw the thing away, before it endangered his life here.

Decision made, Sofia waited until Judith had gone to the bathroom. Then, nightclothes in hand, Sofia tiptoed down the hall. She could hear male voices coming from behind the door at the end of the hall. Sofia walked towards the sound, and tiptoeing, pressed her ear to the door. A child laughed, and then a deeper voice. Was that Samuel? Then came the steady tread of footsteps. Sofia jumped back from the door just in time to see it swing open. Samuel stepped out, the top of his shirt undone and his suspenders hanging around his waist.

"Sofia!" he exclaimed, his face drawing into a broad grin upon seeing her. "Are you lost? You shouldn't be wandering around the halls at night."

"I wanted to speak with you," Sofia said. "Privately, if possible."

"It's really not proper," Samuel said, but he shut the door behind him. "I'll show you to your room."

"Samuel, where did you put that thing?"

"What thing?"

"From where you took me yesterday. From the car. You can't keep it here. Please, just throw it away."

"God, but I wish people would trust me," Samuel said, thrusting his hands into his pockets. "I'm not so foolish as people seem to think. And I'm no child, taking his first steps into the world."

"I don't think you are," Sofia said. She stopped and placed a hand onto his forearm. He wasn't as tall as Abram, though he stood half a head taller than her. She imagined if they hugged, his chin would rest comfortably atop her head. "I just...I don't like those things. They haunt my dreams, and you can't take anything back once it's fired. I may not have your faith, but I do believe that God, wherever he might be, will find other ways to protect us."

"Do you believe God protected you, when he allowed you to be taken by those men and used so thoroughly that you've buried everything about yourself?"

Sofia's mouth was dry. Had God protected her? Certainly, He had in her escape, in the friends that she had found here. But why would He allow her to be taken in the first place? Why would a loving God allow her memories to remain hidden from herself even, and for so long?

"I don't know," Sofia said.

Samuel turned to face her, sandwiching her between him and the wall. He stepped closer to her, enough so that she could smell the sweaty musk of him. "Kiss me," he said.

A tendril of—was it desire, fear, or anticipation—curled in Sofia's belly. From the neighboring rooms came the small sounds of the household preparing to sleep. Sofia glanced to her left, then right, afraid someone might emerge and catch them in this ambiguous position. "We shouldn't," she said. "Not in your mother's house."

"Forget my mother. Soon I will be a man, and I need to know..." Samuel took a breath through his teeth and then stepped back. "I'm so sorry," he said, the words tumbling one after the other like a house of children's blocks collapsing from the base. "I've frightened you. That's not what I meant to do."

"You haven't frightened me," Sofia said. What she felt definitely was not fear. Maybe desire, or perhaps curiosity. If they did this, now, it would be her first kiss, at least in this abbreviated life she'd created. Unlike with Abram, Sofia could touch Samuel without fear of destroying him. In fact, perhaps it was the isolation Samuel felt that led him to this incredible confusion. As far as she was concerned, Samuel was a man. He might even be older than her. "You can, if you like," Sofia said.

Samuel stared at her, his gaze so focused that Sofia felt she might melt in it. Then he rubbed his broad hand over his eyes and said, "I can't."

Outside, the rooster gave a ferocious, terrifying shriek.

CHAPTER 6

It had been a beautiful day, with only a few fluffy clouds high in the stratosphere to blemish the endless sky. Now, the sun had lowered in the sky as afternoon descended. Abram figured it would be around dinnertime by the time he returned to Esther's home. Ruthie would be exhausted tonight, Abram mused, as she had done more work today than in the weeks prior. In general, Abram only took his buggy out to go to church, or sometimes to the nearby grocery store for basic food shopping.

When Abram reached the turnoff to Annie's house, there were no false cops guarding the road, and Abram drove his buggy easily up the path towards her front door. A circular line of hanging wash was suspended between the side of Annie's house and along poles that were connected to a large oak tree. There, sheets and clothing fluttered in the breeze. The women had long since finished their washing and hanging, and now they sat on the porch sipping at juice or lemonade in large red plastic cups.

Isaac ran towards Abram's buggy. His feet were bare and his hat hung by a string over his shoulders, bouncing at his back with each stride. "Hello!" he yelled, waving. "Mamm, it's Abram and Ruthie!"

Annie stood on the porch. Abram stopped Ruthie at the front of Annie's home. Ruthie stamped at the ground with her hooves, her ears flicking back at the noise of Abram's movements as he climbed down from the buggy. "Do you mind seeing if there's some grain for my girl," Abram said, rubbing his palm gently over Ruthie's side. A layer of damp sweat clung to her coat. "And some water. I wish I had time to unhitch her and let her walk around, but once I make this call I'll have to be back to Esther's."

"Esther's? Is that where Samuel took the Englischer girl?"

"It's complicated," Abram said. "Whatever you do, don't let that Maglione or his partner know where she is. I need to call the regular police."

"You think these two have broken the law," Annie said. She waved Abram to walk beside her as Isaac ran to get a bucket for Ruthie.

Abram said, "I think they're not really police officers, and I think they had something to do with Sofia's injuries."

"My God!" Annie brought her hand up to rest on her collarbone. "I was the one who called them."

"Esther suggested we call the Lancaster police and suggest that there may be imposters pretending to be police officers. That way at least the police are aware of the problem."

"Wouldn't it make more sense for the Englischer girl to tell them the story herself?"

"She's too scared to come back here. And she says she can't know for sure," Abram explained. "She never saw their faces."

They climbed the steps onto Annie's porch. Annie's two youngest daughters lay at each edge of the deck, their feet dangling over the edge. They waved as Abram approached. Miriam. Annie's second born rocked gently back and forth on the porch swing by the door. She waved at Abram and said, "Lemonade?" and held up her glass. Condensation clung to the outside. A large chunk of ice had been chipped from the ice-box to cool the drink. It clinked as the girl held the glass to her lips and took a long gulp.

"When I'm finished," Abram said, noting for the first time the dryness of his mouth.

"Oh, give us each one now," Annie said. "It won't hurt to wait another minute before trying the phone."

A pitcher sat in the center of a three-legged stool on the right side of the deck. Miriam took two cups, walked to it, and poured the lemonade. When she had handed one to each of them, Abram took a large gulp. It was fresh, a medley of sweet and tart that Abram found incredibly refreshing.

When Abram had finished half of the glass, Annie put her cup atop the stool and said, "So the Englischer girl's getting her memories back. That's a good thing."

"A few of her memories at least. I think she's so terrified that she doesn't really want to face them, but with time, gentle attention, and God's help, she will feel comfortable enough to remember."

"I hope so. No one wants to live as half of a person. We need our past in order to form our future," Annie said.

Abram finished the lemonade in two large swallows. "I'd best call. If these men are posing as police officers, even if they aren't responsible for what happened to Sofia, it's still a problem."

Annie held out her hand for his glass. "I'll just put this in the kitchen while you're using the phone."

Having no direct number, Abram simply dialed 911. He realized he'd never dialed for the police. The midwife had called for the ambulance when she realized the birthing complications were beyond her skills. And when the ambulance came, it was already too late. Later, he had one brief conversation with a police officer, but he could hardly remember what he'd said, only that the officer had been a Black woman who had promised to pray for him.

"Please state the nature of the emergency," the dispatcher said.

Abram's mouth was dry as he spoke, and his voice croaked as he tried to speak. He coughed, clearing his throat and said, "I think there are two men posing as police officers in my area."

"Posing as police officers? You're calling from Lancaster right? Are you sure this isn't some kind of college prank. Students often use the campgrounds this time of year."

"They seem old for students," Abram said. "And they've come to a number of houses in our area asking about a missing woman. The officer identified himself as Officer Michael Maglione. And he gave us a phone number."

"Okay, I'm going to connect you directly to the Lancaster office. Just stay on the line."

The phone clicked into silence. Abram waited. After about another minute there came another clicking sound and then a woman's voice came through the receiver. "This is Officer Barrett. I hear you're having trouble with two men posing as officers of the law?"

"Yes."

"This is the first complaint we've had of this. And you're sure it's not students playing a prank."

"I'm sure."

"Well, students or no, we can't have that sort of nonsense. You told the 911 dispatcher that one of these men had given you a name and phone number. Can you tell that to me again?"

Abram repeated the information, and answered the follow up questions, doing his best to describe both men as clearly and accurately as possible. When he had finished, Officer Barrett said, "That's very helpful. We'll keep an eye out for these two, and send a patrol car to drive through your area a few times tonight."

"Thank you." Abram ventured, "And you've heard nothing of this missing girl they're talking about?"

"Sofia Angelis? Let me look that name up." There was a long pause, breathing over the phone and the sound of fingers clicking over a keyboard. "Don't see anything, though it takes 48 hours for a report to hit the system for an adult. To be honest, if it wasn't for your description of the firearm, I'd just assume this was some sort of prank. But even so, we don't take kindly to people impersonating an officer of the law. I've put out an APB for two men fitting your description, and we'll be certain to have someone come around and warn people about trusting anyone fitting that description."

"Thank you officer," Abram said.

"No problem," Officer Barrett responded. "Serve and protect, that's the oath I swore. You take care now."

With that, there was another click as the call ended. Judging by how deep the dirt had been ingrained in Sofia's clothing, Abram guessed she'd been missing for at least a few days. It bothered him that Sofia's loved ones, whoever they might be, hadn't noticed quickly enough to even inform the police when she disappeared. Did she have no one who truly cared for her?

Abram placed the phone gently back on the cradle. This had all become so complicated, and Abram couldn't be sure of his place in all of it. Yes, he was attracted to Sofia, but he wouldn't act upon it, not with her being a shell of herself. And yet, it was as if from the moment she had stepped onto his farm with her bruises and torn clothing, her presence had rekindled his interest in life. The red of the phone mounted against the wall seemed richer, and the smell of the fields through the open windows seemed sweeter than they had mere days ago.

God had placed Sofia in Abram's life for a reason, and Abram would do everything in his power to help her. Not as an atonement for how he had failed with Rebekah and not even for the feel of her soft body in his arms. More than anything, Abram wanted Sofia to return to herself. He had faith that this small piece of her that he saw now would only become deeper and more beautiful as her memories returned. In that wish clung a small, irrational hope that she might then come to him, and in seeing each other whole, they might come again to each other.

CHAPTER 7

It had been a beautiful day, with only a few fluffy clouds high in the stratosphere to blemish the endless sky. Now, the sun had lowered in the sky as afternoon descended. Abram figured it would be around dinnertime by the time he returned to Esther's home. Ruthie would be exhausted tonight, Abram mused, as she had done more work today than in the weeks prior. In general, Abram only took his buggy out to go to church, or sometimes to the nearby grocery store for basic food shopping.

When Abram reached the turnoff to Annie's house, there were no false cops guarding the road, and Abram drove his buggy easily up the path towards her front door. A circular line of hanging wash was suspended between the side of Annie's house and along poles that were connected to a large oak tree. There, sheets and clothing fluttered in the breeze. The women had long since finished their washing and hanging, and now they sat on the porch sipping at juice or lemonade in large red plastic cups.

Isaac ran towards Abram's buggy. His feet were bare and his hat hung by a string over his shoulders, bouncing at his back with each stride. "Hello!" he yelled, waving. "Mamm, it's Abram and Ruthie!"

Annie stood on the porch. Abram stopped Ruthie at the front of Annie's home. Ruthie stamped at the ground with her hooves, her ears flicking back at the noise of Abram's movements as he climbed down from the buggy. "Do you mind seeing if there's some grain for my girl," Abram said, rubbing his palm gently over Ruthie's side. A layer of damp sweat clung to her coat. "And some water. I wish I had time to unhitch her and let her walk around, but once I make this call I'll have to be back to Esther's."

"Esther's? Is that where Samuel took the Englischer girl?"

"It's complicated," Abram said. "Whatever you do, don't let that Maglione or his partner know where she is. I need to call the regular police."

"You think these two have broken the law," Annie said. She waved Abram to walk beside her as Isaac ran to get a bucket for Ruthie.

Abram said, "I think they're not really police officers, and I think they had something to do with Sofia's injuries."

"My God!" Annie brought her hand up to rest on her collarbone. "I was the one who called them."

"Esther suggested we call the Lancaster police and suggest that there may be imposters pretending to be police officers. That way at least the police are aware of the problem."

"Wouldn't it make more sense for the Englischer girl to tell them the story herself?"

"She's too scared to come back here. And she says she can't know for sure," Abram explained. "She never saw their faces."

They climbed the steps onto Annie's porch. Annie's two youngest daughters lay at each edge of the deck, their feet dangling over the edge. They waved as Abram approached. Miriam. Annie's second born rocked gently back and forth on the porch swing by the door. She waved at Abram and said, "Lemonade?" and held up her glass. Condensation clung to the outside. A large chunk of ice had been chipped from the ice-box to cool the drink. It clinked as the girl held the glass to her lips and took a long gulp.

"When I'm finished," Abram said, noting for the first time the dryness of his mouth.

"Oh, give us each one now," Annie said. "It won't hurt to wait another minute before trying the phone."

A pitcher sat in the center of a three-legged stool on the right side of the deck. Miriam took two cups, walked to it, and poured the lemonade. When she had handed one to each of them, Abram took a large gulp. It was fresh, a medley of sweet and tart that Abram found incredibly refreshing.

When Abram had finished half of the glass, Annie put her cup atop the stool and said, "So the Englischer girl's getting her memories back. That's a good thing."

"A few of her memories at least. I think she's so terrified that she doesn't really want to face them, but with time, gentle attention, and God's help, she will feel comfortable enough to remember."

"I hope so. No one wants to live as half of a person. We need our past in order to form our future," Annie said.

Abram finished the lemonade in two large swallows. "I'd best call. If these men are posing as police officers, even if they aren't responsible for what happened to Sofia, it's still a problem."

Annie held out her hand for his glass. "I'll just put this in the kitchen while you're using the phone."

Having no direct number, Abram simply dialed 911. He realized he'd never dialed for the police. The midwife had called for the ambulance when she realized the birthing complications were beyond her skills. And when the ambulance came, it was already too late. Later, he had one brief conversation with a police officer, but he could hardly remember what he'd said, only that the officer had been a Black woman who had promised to pray for him.

"Please state the nature of the emergency," the dispatcher said.

Abram's mouth was dry as he spoke, and his voice croaked as he tried to speak. He coughed, clearing his throat and said, "I think there are two men posing as police officers in my area."

"Posing as police officers? You're calling from Lancaster right? Are you sure this isn't some kind of college prank. Students often use the campgrounds this time of year."

"They seem old for students," Abram said. "And they've come to a number of houses in our area asking about a missing woman. The officer identified himself as Officer Michael Maglione. And he gave us a phone number."

"Okay, I'm going to connect you directly to the Lancaster office. Just stay on the line."

The phone clicked into silence. Abram waited. After about another minute there came another clicking sound and then a woman's voice came through the receiver. "This is Officer Barrett. I hear you're having trouble with two men posing as officers of the law?"

"Yes."

"This is the first complaint we've had of this. And you're sure it's not students playing a prank."

"I'm sure."

"Well, students or no, we can't have that sort of nonsense. You told the 911 dispatcher that one of these men had given you a name and phone number. Can you tell that to me again?"

Abram repeated the information, and answered the follow up questions, doing his best to describe both men as clearly and accurately as possible. When he had finished, Officer Barrett said, "That's very helpful. We'll keep an eye out for these two, and send a patrol car to drive through your area a few times tonight."

"Thank you." Abram ventured, "And you've heard nothing of this missing girl they're talking about?"

"Sofia Angelis? Let me look that name up." There was a long pause, breathing over the phone and the sound of fingers clicking over a keyboard. "Don't see anything, though it takes 48 hours for a report to hit the system for an adult. To be honest, if it wasn't for your description of the firearm, I'd just assume this was some sort of prank. But even so, we don't take kindly to people impersonating an officer of the law. I've put out an APB for two men fitting your description, and we'll be certain to have someone come around and warn people about trusting anyone fitting that description."

"Thank you officer," Abram said.

"No problem," Officer Barrett responded. "Serve and protect, that's the oath I swore. You take care now."

With that, there was another click as the call ended. Judging by how deep the dirt had been ingrained in Sofia's clothing, Abram guessed she'd been missing for at least a few days. It bothered him that Sofia's loved ones, whoever they might be, hadn't noticed quickly enough to even inform the police when she disappeared. Did she have no one who truly cared for her?

Abram placed the phone gently back on the cradle. This had all become so complicated, and Abram couldn't be sure of his place in all of it. Yes, he was attracted to Sofia, but he wouldn't act upon it, not with her being a shell of herself. And yet, it was as if from the moment she had stepped onto his farm with her bruises and torn clothing, her presence had rekindled his interest in life. The red of the phone mounted against the wall seemed richer, and the smell of the fields through the open windows seemed sweeter than they had mere days ago.

God had placed Sofia in Abram's life for a reason, and Abram would do everything in his power to help her. Not as an atonement for how he had failed with Rebekah and not even for the feel of her soft body in his arms. More than anything, Abram wanted Sofia to return to herself. He had faith that this small piece of her that he saw now would only become deeper and more beautiful as her memories returned. In that wish clung a small, irrational hope that she might then come to him, and in seeing each other whole, they might come again to each other.

CHAPTER 8

Tailing a horse drawn buggy all over Lancaster County in a stolen, 1979 Buick Skylark was not an easy task.

"It's just a good thing these main roads don't spin off in different directions," D said, after stopping for the third time behind a tree to let the buggy maintain its place five car lengths ahead. "Shame we can't pass though, since he's seen the car."

While they were pulled-over, another car passed and in the distance, the buggy turned left onto a smaller road. D waited a bit more before cruising by. The road was narrow but straight, thankfully, and it lead through a cornfield to a farmhouse, which the buggy was pulling up beside.

"We're going to have to pull the car over and walk up," Mike said.

D squinted into the distance and pointed. "Isn't that a dog?"

"Looks like," Mike said. "Still, you're going to have to get close enough to see if he has the girl there."

"Me?" D shook his head. "Why me?"

"He hasn't seen your face. Lose the police jacket. You can always say you're a lost tourist if he sees you. Just keep clear of the dog."

"Right," D didn't look too confident, but he got out and, avoiding the road, walked into the rows of corn. He came running back about ten minutes later. "Our man's off again. If the girl's at his place, he didn't spend much time with her, and he came out with a bunch of clothes, so I'm betting he's going to deliver them to her now."

"Good deal," Mike said. "Let's take the car up beyond that turn. Then we can see if he turns back to where he came or comes towards us, and then we'll follow from there."

Luck was with them in that Abram turned his buggy back the way he'd come. They followed a distance back on the main road, until Abram turned onto a narrower road, and after a few more minutes again onto an even narrower path through what looked like another stupid flourishing cornfield.

"We'll have to leave the car here," Mike said, with regret. He'd hated cornfields since he was nine, and his older brother had taken Mike in his car with three of his drunken friends to a haunted corn maze. Mike had lost the group, or maybe they'd lost him, he didn't know, but he remembered wandering and shouting until he was exhausted, and then sitting on the ground, clutching a rock in his fist and trying not to cry as the wind made the corn whisper like ghosts.

Neither love nor money would make Mike walk through a cornfield at night. He barely managed it now, in the daylight, easing himself through the shadowy rows as quietly as possible. D glanced back at him occasionally as they walked, a concerned expression on his narrow face. Finally they were close enough to see where Abram had parked his buggy, alongside another, across from two women dressed in Amish style. One was older, with a strong, stocky body which came up to the second woman's chin. The second woman was blonde, her braided hair barely touching her shoulders.

"Is that Sofia?" D whispered.

Mike grinned. "Maybe."

"Has to be," D said. "It's Sofia."

"How do you know?"

"She's wearing shoes."

"So?"

"The old woman isn't, and I bet none of the rest of them are either, except the one who was driving the buggy. Amish don't wear shoes when it's hot, usually. I saw it on Law and Order. Or was it CSI..."

Of course D had seen it on one of those shows. Mike said, "Too many people out now to try and grab her, even with the gun. We'll have to wait until they're sleeping. Do Amish people lock their houses?"

"Maybe..." D shrugged. "Dunno. Probably not."

Well, they'd cross that mountain when they got there, Mike thought, philosophically. Abram and Sofia seemed to have gotten pretty close, in such a short time, judging by how they'd been standing. Lucky guy. Shame Mike couldn't grow a decent crop of facial hair. Guys with beards got all the play.

"We have to move the car again, before he drives back," Mike said. He pointed towards the hen house. A road ran behind it, wide enough, barely, for a buggy to pass. "Let's figure out where that road lets out, and we'll pull up to it and come in the back way." This also had the benefit of avoiding the cornfields, which made it, in Mike's mind, the only viable plan.

"Okay," D said, "But let's get lunch first, and milkshakes. And you should check on Carl."

"Why? Last time I called he was out of it. They said they needed to monitor his bowels so they're keeping him through Monday or at least until he's managed to take a..."

"So you didn't tell him about Sofia?"

"I like my toes on my feet, thank you very much. Anyway, we'll have her back tonight. Why confuse things."

They spent the next few hours filling the car with fast food and driving in circles around Lancaster. It was at times like this Mike wished he had a smart phone. Humans were meant to build in grids, with paved roads moving in straight lines between them. This chaos of fields and gardens and winding dirt roads was unnatural, or if not unnatural, at least wrong. It was about four in the afternoon when they made it to the back road. They sat in the car, eating potato chips, listening to the Christian Rock station, which was the only thing the car radio could receive, and playing word games until the sun set.

"What time do Amish people go to sleep," Mike asked.

D said, "They don't have electricity, so I guess pretty early."

"No help from Law and Order on this one?"

"You don't have to be mean," D said. "You're the one who lost the girl."

"We lost the girl," Mike said. "If you hadn't opened the door while I was talking to her, none of this would have happened."

"How long does it take to give a scared hostage six cans of beans and half a loaf of bread? I thought she'd overpowered you and got the gun somehow. I couldn't just leave you like that. Never leave a man behind."

"We are *not* the Marines."

"Hmmmph." D shoved a cold French fry in his mouth.

After another hour, Mike said, "Now looks good."

There were no lights on the path, but the moon was near full and bright on the dirt path. Mike was careful to keep himself as far from the cornfields as possible. At least the air was still, so instead of ghostly whispering, the cornfields merely stood baleful watch over the dark spaces between their rows. If it wasn't for the fence around the hen house, they might have missed the main house entirely, its form swallowed by the fields that surrounded it.

"Be easier to cut through this corn here than jump the fence 'round that hen house," D whispered.

"I'm not walking through no corn," Mike said, a bit too loudly though forcefully enough. "Forget it."

They approached the fence, wooden posts with wire strung between them to a height just above Mike's waist. On the other side, in front of the hen house door, a chicken slept.

D grabbed at Mike's arm. "I think that's a rooster."

"So?"

"So! Roosters are dangerous!"

Mike stared over the fence at the sleeping rooster, bathed in a circle of moonlight. It might stand as tall as his knee, from claws to fluffy bits on top, and its chicken wings were clipped so it couldn't fly. Mike said, "I think I can take it."

"And they're loud."

"Give me your jacket," Mike said. "And the rest of that bag of cornchips in your pocket. One or the other should shut it up."

D stripped off the jacket and handed Mike a crumpled bag of Tostitos. "I'm going around the long way."

"What happened to Semper Fi?"

"We're not Marines," D said, his tone so bland, Mike couldn't determine if it was sarcasm or a genuine statement of the obvious. Not that it mattered. Tying the jacket around his waist before placing his palms on either side of the largest post, Mike vaulted over the fence.

CHAPTER 9

Samuel shoved Sofia against the wall. "Don't move," he ordered, and then ran down the hallway towards his room. From either side of Sofia, people were opening their doors.

"What's gotten into that ol' rooster now?" Esther asked. Her hair was loose, and she wore a long, cream nightgown. Her feet were bare. "You all stay here, I'll go check on things," she said.

Mary darted out of the room from behind Esther and ran down the hallway towards the window at the end of the hall in front of Samuel's room. She pressed her forehead against the glass. "There's a man out there, with the rooster! Silly Englischer!" she laughed. "He's really running. Maybe we should help him?"

"No!" Samuel burst out of his room. He grabbed Mary up by the waist and carried her away from the window. "Those men are dangerous. You all stay here." He jogged back down the hallway to the staircase, the shape of the gun visible beneath the fabric of his nightshirt. Esther ran after, and Sofia behind, more terrified of what Samuel might do with the gun than of the men who had attacked her. This was worse than the dreams of that noise, the running, blood and pain. These were good people, and simply by being here, she had brought fear and violence into their lives.

God, Sofia prayed desperately as she ran, *please protect Samuel from himself. Don't let him sacrifice everything he cares about for me.*

In the fenced in area in front of the hen-house, the man from Sofia's nightmares ran in circles, waving a jacket at the rooster, who was leaping, flapping and clawing at his face with ruthless abandon. The rooster screamed, and the man shouted curses back, his pants ripped at the knees while deep gouges from the rooster's claws and beak marred his hands and wrists.

"Get away from here!" Samuel shouted. "You're not going to take her!"

"You get this horrible thing away from me!" the man screamed and cursed again. He managed to throw the jacket over the rooster's head, tangling the rooster in a mess of fabric and claws. Seeing an opening, the giant man leaped the fence and ran towards Sofia. "All I want is the girl."

Samuel drew the gun and placed himself in the path of the charging man. "No."

"Samuel!" Esther screamed. "Dear God, no."

At that moment, an arm grabbed Sofia from behind and the cold metal barrel of a gun was shoved into back. "Come with me," a man whispered in her ear. "You don't want to do anything they might regret."

Terrified, Sofia froze. She couldn't breathe. Spots floated in front of her eyes and her skin chilled. "Don't hurt them," Sofia whispered. "Please."

"I don't want to hurt anyone," the man said, his breath tickling her ear. "Now we're going to back up, slowly, okay?"

As though Sofia was going to argue with this choice of kidnapping technique. What was he going to do with her once he'd gotten her away from the farm? Kill her? She wanted to pray to God to save her, but she felt she had spent her coin in prayer on Samuel's behalf, and what had that gotten him? Samuel's grip on the gun was steady, and as Sofia followed the tug of her captor, shuffling sideways and backwards, the profile of Samuel's face in the moonlight came clear.

"Sofia?" Mary's tremulous voice called from just inside the front door. "Who's that man? Where are you going?"

"Go inside, Mary." Sofia said, her voice taut with fear. "I'm fine."

"Sofia?" Samuel kept his gun pointed towards the intruder. "What's going on?"

The intruder stopped three strides from Samuel, and hands in the air said, "Okay, okay, I'm leaving." He took a step back. "Scouts honor."

"Sofia?" Samuel said again.

"There's another Englischer man hugging her from the back and Miss Sofia doesn't look happy," Mary explained.

At that moment, Esther dropped to her knees. "Dear Lord," she shouted, "Save my oldest son from the sin he is about to commit, the blood of another man's soul on his hands, and Dear God, save these men from the horrors they have wrought and may wreak on our Sofia, this poor lost soul who has sought your shelter in my home. Dear God, I am lost. Dear God," she sobbed, her hands clasped at her chin. "Dear God, I cannot understand your infinite wisdom, I can only turn to you in my need, and pray that you make a way."

"Tell her to be quiet," the large man in front of Samuel shouted. "Tell her to shut up!"

The gun barrel shook. Samuel kept it on the intruder as he turned his head to his mother. "Mamm?" His face seemed to crumble into itself.

"Mamm!"

Sofia froze, shocked at the display of Esther's absolute faith. Where before Sofia had been filled with fear, now there was only awe at the strength of this woman.

Esther kept her eyes closed and her head bowed. "Dear God, please help us."

"Make that woman shut up!"

Sofia stopped.

"Move," the man holding her tugged her back, but Sofia bent her knees and held her place. The man sounded a bit desperate now, "Just move, please."

"No," Sofia said. "You're going to have to kill me."

"D, let's go," the other man shouted. "And I swear by God, if you don't shut up lady, my friend is going to shoot your precious guest."

Samuel said. "Do it and I'll kill you."

"No, you won't!" Sofia said.

Esther prayed, "Dear God, please make a way. Please protect my children and these men who are your children from the wrongs they may commit, now and in the future, knowing that in your wisdom and infinite love that the true path will be found."

Sofia closed her eyes and bent her knees, determined she would not move another inch. "Dear God," she prayed. "Give me strength. Please."

The grip on Sofia's body loosened. She kept her eyes closed, her mind focused on her prayer, as the man behind her said. "Forget this, Mike. I'm going home."

"D! Are you insane? We got her!"

"Amnesia or no, get any one of these people on a witness stand and we're going to jail...forever. I'll take my chances with Carl." D patted Sofia awkwardly on the shoulder. "Sorry about this, well, everything. Really, uhh...goodbye."

D turned and walked towards the cornfield. Esther still knelt, her head bowed, the murmur of prayer on her lips. Mike looked at Samuel, then at the cornfield and cursed. Then with more speed than one would expect of a man his size, Mike ran back to the fence enclosing the hen house, vaulted it, and crossing the open space with the angry rooster at his heels, jumped the fence on the other side and was gone.

"Amen," Esther said.

"Mamm? Sofia?" Samuel lowered the gun. "Are you okay?"

Esther said, "Sofia, child, come here."

Sofia walked to Esther and dropped to her side. "I'm fine," she said to both of them. "Esther, that has to be the bravest thing I've ever seen."

"So you've gotten your memories back then?"

Sofia blinked, "No..." though she wondered now if it could even matter.

"I mean, nothing yet."

"Then that's cursing me with faint praise, ja," Esther laughed, a high pitched sound tinged with hysteria. Tears rolled down her face, wetting her cheeks. "Thank you, God."

"Mamm," Samuel took a step towards his mother, then stopped. "I wasn't going to...I mean, I couldn't let them take Sofia. You saw what they did to her." Samuel's lower lip was trembling like a child's.

"I need you to take that thing away," Esther said. "It's one thing to have a gun to shoot for food or for pests, but that is meant only to kill other human beings. I want it out of my house."

"If I hadn't stopped them, they'd have taken Sofia and done who knows what to her. What was I supposed to do?"

"For all others have spoken of the length you've taken to make your choice and how I've not done enough to force you to make a decision, that I've indulged your frivolity, I've never had reason to be ashamed of you until this day. Your father..." Esther closed her eyes, as though the pain of looking at her son was too much to bear. "It is better your father didn't see this. Now take that thing away." With that, Esther stood, and taking Sofia's hand in hers said, "Let's go inside. You'll want another bath. Mary!" she shouted. "To bed! And all of you the same. We're hosting church tomorrow."

"Mamm." Samuel's voice caught in a sob.

"And don't return until you've decided to respect our traditions, whether or not you choose to follow them."

.

In God's Hands

Love is patient and kind; love does not envy or boast; it is not arrogant or rude. It does not insist on its own way; it is not irritable or resentful; it does not rejoice at wrongdoing, but rejoices with the truth. Love bears all things, believes all things, hopes all things, endures all things. Love never ends. --Corinthians 13: 4-8

CHAPTER 1

Sofia slept in fits and spurts, interrupted by fragments of memory. Snorkeling over expanses of colorful coral, schools of jewel-like fish flitting beneath her in trickles of displaced water. Perching on the edge of a white sofa in an uncomfortable dress, her toes barely touching the floor as the adults around her chatted about boring things and handed her crème filled wafers when she tried to interrupt. Pungent cigarettes behind the school gym, laughing with other girls. They all mixed together like a handful of puzzle pieces thrown haphazardly on the floor.

And then there was the man. It wasn't dancing now. Instead were more quiet things: sitting on the sofa, throwing popcorn at each other as a movie flickered in the background or sharing a cup of sorbet at a quiet cafe where people at neighboring tables speaking what sounded like Italian.

"Quit teasing," she'd admonished him playfully, "You know my Spanish can't keep up with your Italian."

Had Sofia been in love? Was she still?

When the rooster crowed her to full wakefulness, Sofia was relieved. She sat up, rubbing her eyes. The smell of cinnamon bread seemed to seep up from the floors, and her stomach growled.

"That'd be the Friendship bread for after church," Judith said. "It's the best. So..." she added, with a slight hesitation in her tone, "How are you doing today?"

Sofia wondered how long the other girl had been lying awake, wanting to ask that question.

Judith was a sensitive girl. She seemed to know without asking that the night before with the two men trying to kidnap Sofia, Esther's prayer, Samuel's gun and his being cast out of the house by his mother were all too raw to put into words. Last night, Sofia had just wanted to soak in the tub, the water a bit lukewarm but satisfying, until the feel of that man's hands around her neck had been fully washed away. Now, after a fitful night's sleep, Sofia was still, more than anything, awed by Esther. Assaulted in her home by strangers while her son risked becoming a killer to save them, Esther had fallen to her knees, asking God for guidance and by that had completely diffused the situation. Even if Sofia someday remembered every moment of her life from birth to death with perfect clarity, she doubted she would ever see such a profound or powerful display of faith.

"Sofia?"

"I'm feeling better," Sofia responded. "A bit tired, but looking forward to church."

"The service will be in German," Judith explained. "And our services tend to run a bit longer than Enlischer's I think. We usually go for three to four hours, and have two sermons, which I'm sorry you won't be able to understand, but I'll try to translate for you as best I can."

"Oh, I'd be so grateful," Sofia said. "But only if it's not a disruption. I feel like I've already brought too much trouble into your lives."

"It's not your fault that people decided to hurt you," Judith said. She stood, and crossed the space between their two beds, sitting down beside Sofia. "Evil is evil. I only saw a bit of it from the door though, with Mary. Why were those men after you?"

"I don't know. They mentioned something about a man named Carl, and, I think that before I was very wealthy, so maybe they wanted money."

"That's horrible! I really don't understand the Englischer obsession with money. So much of your music even seems to be about money: getting it, spending it, saving it, this seems a sin to me. I mean, yes, you earn enough for your needs and to contribute to your family and the community, but beyond that, what's the point? Love, the beauty of nature, and your relationship with God, those should be the most important things in your life."

"I don't think most people, well, most Englischers," the word felt awkward on Sofia's tongue, "think the way you do. I don't think I did."

"But now?"

"Your mother, Abram, you, and even Samuel, you're all such good people. I don't think my family was so close."

"What do you remember of them?"

"I think my father must have worked a lot, and my mother was very social because I remember her having people over and it seems like it was a normal thing. I had a nanny, more than one I think, and my parents sent me away to school when I was seven."

"Sent you away!"

Sofia shrugged. "I was home for holidays, I think. I remember swimming in the ocean over the coral."

"Still, that's no replacement for a proper home."

Sofia wished she had more of an ability to judge that. She'd gotten the impression of herself as a child, serious, studious, and desperate for acceptance. If her family prayed, Sofia didn't remember it. But there was so much she didn't remember. Her memories were returning to her at night in dribs and drabs, and like dreams, they faded as the sun rose. Sofia wasn't even sure she wanted them. A plain life would suit her, she imagined. But what if there were people looking for her? Her two captors had been convinced that someone would pay a good amount of money to see her again. If she had family or a lover who were worried about her, she was only making them suffer more by not letting the legitimate authorities know that she was alive and safe.

"I should call the police," Sofia said. "Now that I know those guys aren't after me anymore."

"That's good, but it will have to be after church," Judith explained. "The entire district will be here, so you won't be able to use anyone's house or telephone. After the service, you can always go back to Annie's with her family. That will be for the best."

Relieved that she wasn't being any more negligent to a family she could barely remember, Sofia's heart lightened and she smiled. "I'm excited to see your service. I guess there are some things we have to do to prepare."

"Well, most of the cooking has already been done, and the Bishop will be by with the benches and songbooks for everyone, so it's just getting the water ready for the horses, which is men's business. Samuel does..." Judith bit her lip. "I suppose I'll have to help get the younger boys in line for that."

"I'm sorry," Sofia said, twisting her waist to face the younger woman and taking her hands. "It's my fault."

"Not unless you gave him that thing and asked him to bring it—you didn't, did you?"

"I begged him not to when he showed it to me."

"Then it's not your fault. Samuel can make his own decisions." Judith extricated herself from Sofia's grip. "Come on, we have to get water and grain for the horses, not to mention checking on the hens, though they're probably so agitated who knows if they managed to lay. And there's the cows..."

Judith rattled on as she moved around the room, making her bed and braiding her hair. Sofia followed suit. When they'd finished putting the room in order, Judith said, "You'll want to use the bathroom and brush your teeth. Then we'll have breakfast and wait for the church wagon so we can set up the room."

"Do you always have church services in your house?"

Judith laughed, "Heaven's no! Hosting church is a fair amount of work, so it rotates. Usually we use a home, but sometimes for the smaller houses, a barn is easier. You Englischers usually have a building for it, but we believe that the church is the people, so it's better not to get too attached to any one place, ja."

"That sounds lovely," Sofia said. And it made sense. If there were no worshipers, then the church would be nothing more than a large, pretty building. So many things about the Amish faith appealed to Sofia. She loved the closeness that people shared with each other and the deep security they had in their relationship with God. Even in the face of loss or fear, they knew where they stood, and even when they struggled, they also found their way.

Sofia braided her hair and put on another of Judith's dresses, this one also dark blue with a cream colored apron tied around her waist. Judith wore shoes with thin, white socks. Sofia did the same, stuffing an extra pair in the toes of her borrowed shoes, the only thing she had left of Abram's gift. Esther had taken the rest of the clothes Abram had given her before bed with a declaration that it would be best to donate them to the congregation. Sofia had agreed, but she found herself feeling a bit more lost without those comforting bits of fabric.

Sofia admitted to herself at least that she was looking forward to seeing Abram, not only for the news he might offer from his call to the police about her own kidnapping, but also just because she missed him. It felt like more than a developing friendship when they'd embraced. But who was she to attach so much meaning to a mere hug? Maybe Abram was simply being kind. And if Abram did feel something too, she couldn't toy with his heart without knowing her own life. Who was that man in her dream, and why had they seemed to know each other so intimately?

Cleaning her teeth in the tiny bathroom mirror, Sofia had wanted the array of cosmetics she'd had in her dreams and make herself beautiful. She wanted to make a good impression on everyone. Also, if she was being honest with herself, she wanted to impress Abram. But then he'd already seen her at her worst, bruised and bloody, so really, painting her face with cosmetics would only make her seem ridiculous and false. Still she took extra care to smooth her hair and retied her apron so that it was straight and gave hint to the shape of her figure beneath.

Judith's lips twitched with some hidden mirth when Sofia returned, dressed for the day, and Sofia averted her gaze. They busied themselves with eating breakfast and then preparations through dawn. Sofia was kept so busy, cutting vegetables, arranging benches, and moving trays of food for storage until after the ceremony that she barely had time to glance at the buggies as they lined up along the cow's field for the service. They'd moved most of the furniture out of the living room the previous day, and the benches were then arranged in rows from opposite walls with a space between for the preacher to speak. The day was already warm, and all of the windows in the room had been opened, filling the air with the smell of the fields and a cooling breeze. When the old grandfather clock in the kitchen struck nine, the women seated themselves on the benches to the left of the open space.

All of the women were in muted, dark colors, but only Esther and an elderly woman whose braids were thin weaves of dark gray, wore black. As Esther bustled between and through the other women, many stole glances at her, and though Sofia couldn't understand their language, as they whispered to each other she thought she heard Samuel's name and the word rumspringa, scattered inside their words.

Annie greeted her with a warm hug, and said that Abram had called the police, prompting Sofia to give a much abbreviated explanation of the previous night's events.

"My God!" Annie exclaimed when Sofia had finished, her right hand clutching at her collarbone in her surprise. "At least you're safe now. Do you think these two men will be returning?"

"No," Sofia said. "But if it's okay, I'd like to use your phone tonight to call the police."

"Ja! Of course."

Esther called for Annie from the kitchen, and the plump woman handed Sofia the tray she'd been carrying and shouted, "I'm coming!"

Judith came back inside the house as the women were seating themselves, the hem of her dress dusty and damp from where she had been helping water the horses. She waved Sofia over. Relieved, Sofia sat next to the younger woman. Along every few feet on the benches were old, weathered books with frayed leather binding and thick paper covers with the word Ausbund written on them in faded calligraphy. At first, Sofia had thought they might be Bibles, but flipping through the pages she guessed it was either a book of poetry or perhaps songs, like the ones the young people had been singing at the singing circle two nights and a lifetime ago.

Once Judith had called her over, a few of the other girls gave Sofia shy smiles which Sofia returned with gratitude. Mary and another girl, a dark-haired girl with a serious face belied by her habit of tapping Mary on the opposite shoulder and then giggling into her hand whenever Mary tried to figure out who had poked her, ran between the older women and younger girls, handing them songbooks and chattering with obvious joy. Mary's friend had a doll cradled in her arms, while Mary had what looked like a sketchpad shoved inside the band of her apron. With the services being three hours long, Sofia wasn't surprised that the girls needed some means to entertain themselves, despite understanding the language.

The girls drifted back to their mothers as the men filed in. The men sat across from the women, the oldest entering first and seating themselves in the front while the younger men sat further back. Sofia searched for Abram in the throng. He was almost the final bearded man to come in, and he kept his gaze fixed firmly in front of him as he searched for a place to sit. Sofia stifled disappointment. Why would he be looking for her? She was no longer his responsibility. At this point, all they had in common were the too-large shoes on her feet, and that was a reminder of loss, not joy.

The last to enter were the young men, their faces not yet shaved, followed by the young boys.

"Why don't the young men have beards?" Sofia whispered to Judith in the noise of shuffling boots and fabric of the men taking their places.

"They grow them after they're baptized. Usually from when they get married, but if they take longer for some reason for that, they'll grow their beard anyway. Only children and boys on rumspringa go unshaven." Judith rested her palm on Sofia's forearm and leaned closer and pointed to the front row. "That's the Minister. He'll be giving the sermons. And there's his son!" she pointed to a youth who looked to be about sixteen, sitting in the second to last row. "Isn't he handsome?"

Sofia supposed the young man was. He was tall and thin with a narrow, beardless face, his hair light brown touched with blond. He took a seat in the back, with the other boys who had not yet been baptized.

The Minister stood and spoke.

"He's welcoming everyone to the service," Judith whispered into Sofia's ear. "And now we're going to have a moment of prayer to thank God that we are able to gather here today."

Sofia bowed her head. The prayer went on, and though Sofia couldn't understand the words, the feeling of gratitude from the Minister and the congregation was palpable. She closed her eyes and prayed too, thanking God that he had seen her through these past few days and led her to safety. She also prayed for Samuel, though she wasn't sure precisely what she hoped God would do. She wanted Samuel to live a good life and be happy, to be true to the memory of his father whom he cherished, and hoped that wherever Samuel wound up ultimately, he would be able to reconcile with Esther and his family. Though Sofia knew she hadn't intentionally brought violence and contention to their household, she still felt responsible. She only hoped that now, her prayer would help bring some healing and help to these people who had all been so kind to her.

"Amen," she whispered, when the prayer ended.

Next they opened their songbooks. There was no music written on the pages, only words, but the congregation knew the arrangement well. Two men began, singing a single word in beautiful harmony. Soon others in the congregation joined in. The song began slowly, the words seeming to stretch in an elongated note, but as the song continued, the pace increased, and around her smiles and joy echoed in the faces. Sofia smiled also. The first song drew to a measured close.

"Next is the Loblied," Judith said, "It means praise song."

A pure and beautiful baritone began the song, and Sofia's breath caught as she realized that the singer was Abram.

"My God," Judith breathed. "He hasn't led a song since his wife died."

Abram stood, drawing the note out. A lump grew in Sofia's throat as she watched him. His face had a sincere focus and while he didn't smile, his eyes shone with something deeper than mere happiness. Singing was his joy, Sofia realized, and within the music, he was beautiful. The other men joined in, their voices weaving with Abram's. Though Abram's voice was by far the most powerful, the others did not weaken his song. Instead, they textured the music, the women's voices soaring above as the men maintained the rhythm. Abram held the final note, his voice fading like the final fingers of sunset fading to night.

Silence.

Abram met Sofia's gaze, and she felt, for a moment, like she was staring into a fire. Not one that destroyed, but one that warmed and nourished. Abram had a burning passion, one that like his voice, had been choked by grief and self-doubt. In this moment though, Sofia wondered how anyone could be touched by that flame and not want to hold it. Irrational jealousy stabbed through her at the thought that any of these other unmarried women on the benches around her might have a greater right to take that. Her face warmed. These were not godly thoughts. They were not thoughts worthy of the gift that Abram had given them, nor the courage he had shown in challenging his grief. Embarrassed, Sofia averted her gaze.

The rest of the service went by in a blur of prayers, preaching, and song. Mary had fallen asleep about halfway through, her head resting in Esther's lap. Some of the young boys in the back also nodded off, and an old man at the front rested his closed eyes on the palms of his hand as the minister preached an hour long sermon. Through the service, Sofia stole glances at Abram. He seemed thoroughly involved in the service, and while he didn't lead any other hymns, he did sing throughout, the beauty and power of his voice easily recognizable from the rest. The service ended with a final prayer, at which point the congregation stood. Many stretched, and the crack of popping joints and conversation sounded through the room.

At this point, the men and women seemed allowed to mingle. Judith grabbed Sofia's hand and said, "You have to come with me to talk to Jacob."

"Jacob?"

"The minister's son. We'll have to introduce you to the minister first. And the Bishop."

"Of course," Sofia said, trying her best not to feel cheated. She would have a chance to speak with Abram before everyone left, she hoped.

So it was another round of introductions, where Sofia did her best to be polite and show her respect for her friends' faith. "The service was beautiful," she said. "Especially the singing. I wish I could have understood more, though Judith did a wonderful job of translating for me."

"We're very happy to have you with us," the Bishop said. He looked to be about fifty years old with a salt and cinnamon beard and smile lines around his eyes. "Abram has spoken highly of you."

Sofia hoped her joy at the compliment wasn't too obvious on her face. "Thank you. If it's not too much trouble...how does one join your church?"

The Bishop's eyes widened. "I'm sorry, Miss," he said, "But you have to be Amish to be a member of our church."

"Like, born Amish? You don't take converts?"

"Well...um...yes we do accept converts, those who have a genuine change of faith, but in your unique situation..."

"What do you mean?"

"Abram led me to believe you were having some trouble with your memory?"

"Yes. I'm having some dreams of my past, but I can't really remember much about who I was before. I'm going to talk to the police tonight, and then once my family knows I'm safe, I will be able to join without worrying anyone." Sofia did her best not to think of the man in her dream that she had been so intimate with. He might even be a brother, or a friend, though the latter seemed especially unlikely.

The Bishop shook his head. "We Amish require that anyone who chooses to be baptized in our faith do so with a cogent mind and full understanding of what their choice entails. That's one of the key purposes of rumspringa. No matter your intentions, you can't give us a true promise if you don't know yourself fully."

Sofia felt as if someone had ripped the floor out from beneath her feet. The bishop was right. How could she promise to give up the outside world and her own life if she only had the vaguest idea of what that meant, especially the latter. "But when I get my memories back," she asked, "Will I be able to join you, if that's what I want to do?"

"Nothing will give me greater pleasure," the Bishop said, taking both of her hands in his. "I believe you would be an asset to our congregation."

"Excuse me, Bishop Stoltzfus!" A man Sofia didn't know tapped the Bishop on the shoulder.

"Good day, Miss Sofia," the Bishop said. Sofia wished him a good day as well, and stepped back to leave the Bishop room to speak to the next person who needed his attention.

Judith linked her arm inside Sofia's limp one. "Come, we have to make sure we get our shift for lunch."

"Yes," Sofia said, forcing a smile. No matter the truth of the Bishop's words, she didn't want to face her past. Her experience of it so far had been painful and strange. She couldn't imagine being this woman she inhabited in her dreams, this woman who lived in a beautiful yet cold apartment and loved another man.

"Sofia, are you okay?" Judith asked. "What did Bishop Stoltzfus say to you?"

"Only that I need to know myself before I can decide to join you."

"You want to join us!" Judith clapped her hands in front of her chest and gave a little hop. "That's wonderful! I'll teach you our German. You could live with us and maybe Samuel—it doesn't matter, only, we would be happy to have you. Joyful!"

Samuel, yes, how could she have allowed Samuel to slip her mind? Samuel had sacrificed everything he valued in order to protect her, and in turn she was mooning over Abram while allowing her fear of the past to paralyze her. "I need to return to my home for a bit," Sofia said, "and regain my memories, as many as possible, before I can make any serious decisions."

"Yes, of course. But you will come back, right? You will, won't you?"

"If I can," Sofia said. It was the most honest promise she could make.

CHAPTER 2

Esther's words clung to Abram as he entered her home for the church service. No matter how he thought he wanted a deeper relationship with Sofia, he wouldn't impose himself, nor would he treat her as a replacement for Rebekah. Though Abram hadn't fully understood Judith's hurried explanation of the previous night's events as she helped water Ruthie, he recognized that God had protected Sofia. That was enough. Abram was careful to keep his gaze from the women's side of the church, instead taking his seat and staring at the floor between the benches.

When the minister gave the benediction, Abram followed the prayer with a lighter heart than he had since Rebekah's passing. He'd felt so much lighter these past two days. Having Sofia stumble onto his farm had been a gift from God. This morning, when he'd woken on the narrow guest bed, he was able to open his eyes immediately. There was no wrenching loss at finding himself alone. Instead, the spill of sunlight over his pillow seemed a gentle caress, spurring him to movement. The breeze through the open window brought the sweet smell of earth and grass, and at his feet, Johanna stirred and gave a swallowed bark.

The benediction ended, and it felt natural for Abram to start the song. Notes flowed effortlessly. The choked bit of phlegm that had rested in his chest these past two years, blocking all but the simplest sounds, had dissipated, leaving only music behind. Abram reveled in the song, the discipline of holding the notes just so, and the joy that singing had always brought him. When he finished, his eyes opened upon Sofia. She was positively radiant, the gold of her hair braided under her kapp, and her face shining with joy. Their eyes met and Abram knew himself lost. If he'd had any means, he'd have crossed the space between their benches and taken her into his arms.

Sofia flushed, and averted her gaze to the floor. Embarrassed at her discomfort, Abram quickly did the same. He was here to express his gratitude and revel in the glory of God, not inflict his base desires on an unsuspecting stranger. Abram joined in the refrain of the praise song. For the rest of the service, he listened intently, forcing his thoughts back to his love of God whenever they threatened to stray. When the service ended, he let his gaze fall again upon Sofia, but her attention was focused on something Judith was whispering.

It was for the best.

Some of the unbaptized boys went to move the large table so that the benches could be arranged around it and food piled atop it for the luncheon. There wasn't enough room for everyone to eat together, so they had to take shifts. The old men ate first, the old women, after that mothers, and then married men. Last came the young men and children. Men and women didn't eat together, though the women of the house would serve hot coffee and water to all who wanted it when they weren't eating.

Abram fell in step with the other married men heading outside towards the parked buggies, letting conversation wash over him—mostly about the promise of the upcoming meal—with only minimal comment. They stopped beside the church wagon, some leaning against the side while the rest spread out into the road in a loose circle.

A group of children, boys and girls, dashed past towards the chicken coop. Mary, Esther's youngest, lead the group, her hands flying in animated gestures, "and then that 'ol rooster chased that Englischer all..."

Boaz Schrock, a large boned man with a blunt nose and deep set eyes who had been Abram's year-mate through their eighth and final grade, asked, "Has anyone seen Samuel? I expected he'd be at church at least, as he's still got a room at Esther's."

"Endless rumspringa," another of the men said with a snort. "Better he just go and live with the Englischers and be done with it. Or maybe he has. There must be some reason Esther's wearing black."

"Esther's clothing is her business," Abram said sharply. "Judgment ought be left only to the Almighty God, ja."

"Ja." Boaz had the grace to look embarrassed. "Still, it's odd, you must admit. And then there's the Englischer girl she's keeping."

"Sofia needed help. It's Christian charity." Abram shrugged.

"Heard you brought this Sofia to the singing circle at Annie's on Friday. It was all the talk when she ran out with Samuel. And then the police came?"

"Samuel did nothing wrong," Abram said.

Boaz laughed. "You're worse than that dog of yours holding a bone when it comes to sharing news." He kicked the back of his boot into the earth, raising a puff of dust. "Could you at least tell me how you came to meet her, or is that something for you to hold and tease until all the meat is gone?"

"She came to my farm, needing help. She will be returning to her own people as soon as she finds out who they are."

"She doesn't know?"

"She's having some trouble with her memory." Abram folded his arms, leaning his shoulder against the church wagon.

"And that's all you're going to tell us about it, ja." Boaz slapped Abram firmly on the shoulder and laughed again. "It's good to hear you singing again though. Whatever's going on with this Englischer, she's done you good."

"Yes," Abram said.

The subject changed, much to Abram's relief. Soon they were being called into the main room. The smell of food made Abram's stomach growl. On the table was spread a sumptuous feast: fresh baked bread with sweet, green tomato jam, ham and pea salad, beets, pickles, and a giant crock of hot noodle soup, as well as berry pies, cinnamon friendship bread, and molasses cookies with white lemon frosting. Abram took a plate and bowl, and after taking his food, sat at the end of the bench and started to eat.

A cup was placed in front of him. "Coffee?"

"Sofia!"

Sofia grinned. "They said each of us should take a turn serving the drinks. It's good to see you."

Abram's cheeks warmed. "Ja."

"Your singing was really beautiful," Sofia said.

"It's for the joy of God."

"Well, it brought me joy too." Sofia poured the coffee, splashing a few drops on the tablecloth as she lifted the lip of the coffeepot. "I'm sorry!" she said, searching around for a napkin. "I'm so clumsy."

"It's fine."

They both reached for the napkin beside Abram's plate at the same time, his hand clasping over her fingers. They were soft and warm, only a newly healed scar on below the nail of her ring finger disturbing the smoothness of her skin. Abram released her hand. "I'm sorry," he said.

"It's fine." Sofia rested the coffee pot on the table. "May I speak with you later? When I'm not so busy."

"Of course," and there came that spike of joy again, that she had sought out his company.

"Thank you," Sofia said. The warmth of her eyes was like an embrace. She took up the coffeepot again and moved to the next person. Across the table, Boaz met his gaze and nodded before returning to his meal.

CHAPTER 3

Sofia almost hadn't asked Abram to speak afterward, worried that asking to talk with him again alone might be impolite, or worse imposing on his good nature, but it wasn't as though she was there to discuss frivolous things. He had information to share about his call to the police, and Esther had been so busy this morning, Sofia doubted Abram had been able to find the time to get the news from the older woman. So it was with a light heart that Sofia worked her way around the table, giving coffee as needed. The women would eat next, and then teens and young children, Sofia assumed with mothers on hand to supervise.

The food looked so delicious, it made Sofia a bit weak, and she wished that the eating rituals were fairer, though Sofia supposed most of the women had nibbled some before the service and again in the kitchen before taking the trays to the table. She wished she had been close enough with some of them to manage the same. If her memories came back, would she still feel so much like an outsider everywhere she went? But at the same time, as awkward as she sometimes found it here, she couldn't imagine herself making a place amongst the lavish spectacles of her dreams. She liked the simplicity of the homes here, and the measured pace at which people moved, never stopping, but also not pushed in many directions, distracted by the wonders that vied for their attention at every moment. The world of Sofia's dreams seem bright, loud, and cold. She wasn't sure she wanted that. She couldn't imagine that she had ever wanted that.

When the women's time came to eat, Sofia stayed with Judith and the other unmarried women, enjoying their chatter both about Amish concerns and also the parts of Englischer life they were being exposed to. Sofia found herself ruefully shaking her head when song names were mentioned, though she found that if one of them sang a line or two that she could often join in. This was both delightful and a bit scary.

As they were working through dessert—Judith had insisted Sofia have a small taste of every dish, and after molasses cookies and four different types of pie, Sofia was beginning to hate sugar—one of the girls from the singing circle said, "How long has it been since Abram's led one of the songs? It has to be three years at least." She had poker straight hair and a nose to match.

"Ja, Martha, since his wife passed on," Judith said. "But I think he may have found something new," she said, mildly, taking a forkful of strawberry tart into her mouth. "I heard he might be courting Mrs. Bieler."

Sofia's stomach seized. She took a sip of the coffee, though it was too strong and not sweet enough for her taste.

"But she's old!" Martha exclaimed, curling a lock of hair around her index finger.

"Thirty-six this spring. She can still have more children if she remarries soon. It's not good for children to go too long without a father, and her husband died so horribly."

"But Abram's ten years younger."

"Oh!" Judith raised both eyebrows. "So *you're* interested then?"

"No!" Martha shook her head rapidly. "Abram's so...correct all the time..." she wrinkled her nose, "And he doesn't smile."

Sofia didn't want to interrupt, but she felt compelled to defend Abram. "He smiles," she said, and then took another gulp of the coffee.

Martha fixed her gaze on Sofia. "Abram did bring you to the singing circle, but you ran off with Samuel."

"That had nothing to do with Abram," Sofia said. "It was...something else."

"Are you running from the cops?" Martha leaned forward on the table on her elbows with an expression of fascination. "What did you do?"

"Nothing!"

"Leave her alone, Martha." Judith added in a whisper, "Ever since you got your hands on those Englischer novels, I swear!"

"They're interesting." Martha licked her thumb and ran it over her plate, getting the last cookie crumbs before running the napkin across her lower lip. "And Esther's baking is, as always, delicious."

Sofia relaxed, sipping at the too strong coffee as the other girls continued to gossip. The day was a bit warm, and sweat clung to the back of her neck. Once she had finished with her plate, she took it to the kitchen. In the open space of floor between the oven and the far wall sat two large, metal tubs of soapy water. The first held plates and the second cups. A smaller tray sat on the counter, filled halfway with forks, knives, and spoons. Sofia put her dirty dishes into the water and then made her way outside, hoping to catch a glimpse of Abram. The sun was bright, and she had to place a hand over her eyes in order to see.

The children had been herded inside to eat, leaving the older men to chat amongst themselves while the mothers helped the smallest children. Annie was standing by the church wagon, talking with the Bishop. When she saw Sofia, she waved, calling Sofia over.

"Sofia!" she said, drawing the Englischer girl into a tight hug. "I'm so glad you're okay. Esther told me what happened. It must have been so frightening."

"It was, but everyone else was so strong, and they left. I was so amazed!"

"Ja, God listens to all of our prayers, of course, but I think Esther has a special place at his ear. She's a powerful woman, powerful in her faith."

"I'd never imagined anything like that," Sofia said. "But Samuel...what do you think will happen to him?"

"Oh, what happened? Esther's been tight-lipped about the whole situation, for all she's wearing mourning colors. She says she'll only talk about it with the Bishop."

"Oh." Sofia bit the inside of her lip. "Hmm...I shouldn't then. I mean, it's really not for me to tell."

"Yes, right, of course."

"But I was hoping to use your phone," Sofia said. "I'll need to speak with the police directly tomorrow."

"Are you sure it's safe? Those two men..."

"They were pretending," Sofia explained. "But they're gone now. Esther made sure of that. But if I'm to join you, I need to talk to my family, and do my best to regain my memories."

"You want to join us?" Annie's brow furrowed. "Englischers don't often join us."

"I know. The Bishop was very clear. I need to have all of my faculties, and make my decision with a clear mind, but I know where my heart lies. It won't change."

Annie folded her arms over her chest, her expression becoming more serious. "Have you spoken to Abram about this?"

"Not yet," Sofia said.

"Don't," Annie said. "Not until you're sure. The man has been through enough. He's only beginning to come back to himself."

"I'd never hurt him!"

"I don't believe you would want to," Annie said, "But the heart is a strange thing, even when we think we know ourselves completely. Which you don't. So please, be careful."

There was a weight in Sofia's chest, just below her collarbone. The joy she had taken in Abram's touch seemed an illusion, as much an illusion as the dancing Sofia of her dreams. Annie was right. Until she knew herself, until she learned who the man in her dream was who had held her so closely, she had no business further disrupting Abram's world. Especially when he had just begun, whether because of her or through the grace of a higher power, to live again.

"I understand," Sofia said.

Annie nodded, and then taking Sofia by both hands pulled her close. She let go Sofia's hands and wrapped her arms around the smaller girl. "Thank you," Annie whispered.

Sofia closed her eyes and swallowed down the thickness in her throat. She wished the hug didn't feel so much like a goodbye.

CHAPTER 4

It wasn't until Abram had finished helping to load the benches into the church wagon that he had a chance to look for Sofia. She stood on the patio, holding a bundle of clothes and talking to Esther. Abram was loath to interrupt, but most of the other families had hitched their horses to their buggies, and many had started to leave.

"Annie's sister and husband sell baked goods at a market in the city on Wednesdays," Esther was saying. "You can get a ride with her driver then, though it would be best first to contact the police from her house. Or maybe your family will come and pick you up from her house."

Sofia nodded. "But I don't know if there's room in her buggy, what with her husband and children."

"I can take you," Abram said. "It's on my way home."

Sofia cast her gaze downwards. "I wouldn't want to impose."

"It's no imposition," Abram said. In truth, it would be a delight. He'd enjoyed telling her the stories of the farms and the people who lived there, and she'd seemed to enjoy it as well, her face animated as she asked questions and made comments with large, excited gestures. "Besides, it will give me time to tell you about the call I made to the police yesterday, and it would probably be best for me to be around for the call again anyhow."

"Yes, and I should come along too," Esther said. "As I also witnessed these two men and what they tried to do to my home and guest. Sofia and I can ride together in the back."

Esther had a valid point, but as she stared at him, head cocked and eyes narrowed just a bit as though she were preparing to battle a particularly aggressive stain, Abram wondered if she was more interested in chaperoning than any conversation with the police. Abram forced a smile. "Of course, that would be for the best."

So Abram sat alone at the front of the buggy, while the two women rode in the back. When they reached Annie's, Abram tipped his hat to Sofia and Esther, fully expecting to be asked to leave.

"Aren't you coming in with us?" Sofia asked. "The police may want to talk to you too."

"Ja." Abram drove the buggy and stopped it behind Annie's family buggy. After tending to Ruthie, he joined Esther and Sofia, and all three walked towards Annie's house. Annie's husband Mark was on the porch with his feet propped up on the railing. He was solid, with a slight paunch and though his hairline was receding at the temples and salted with gray, his beard was still full and brown. He had a sketchpad on his lap that he was working at with a well-used yellow pencil. Mark looked up as they approached and gave Abram and the two women a warm smile. "Gut-n-owed," he said, wishing them a good evening.

Abram and Esther returned the greeting, and Sofia tried, and the sincerity of her attempt made Mark's smile widen. "Gut! Gut!" he said. "Very good! You must be the Englischer girl Abram found?"

"Yes...uhh...ja," Sofia said, her cheeks reddening. "Abram has been very kind, well, everyone has."

"So you're to use the telephone then? Annie is putting the youngest two to bed, they always get so excited after the service. Seeing all of their friends, ja. I'll walk you in."

Mark closed the pencil inside the sketchbook and accompanied them inside. In the living room, two of the older children were reading by the dying light through the window. In another half-hour it would be dark. Abram hoped to be back on the road by then. Tomorrow, he would have to see to his fields and all of the work he'd let go these past few days since Sofia had come onto his farm and beautifully upset the measured pace of his life.

Abram dialed the emergency line and explained the situation to the operator, who then asked to speak with Sofia.

"Yes," Sofia said. "Yes. No, I'm fine now." She told her story again, and then paused, followed by, "Yes, I'm safe now. No, I don't think these men are coming back. Yes, a sketch artist is fine. How tall am I? Not very." She stared into the air for a moment. "I'm short I guess."

"About five three," Abram interjected.

Sofia shot him a grateful look. "Maybe 5' 3", my friend says. My eyes are hazel and my hair is blonde, but it's darker at the roots. Really! You do?" Her eyes widened and she nodded rapidly "Yes! Please! Will the officer need to speak with Esther also? She was there last night. A half hour then, yes, thank you! I'll give you to Annie's husband for the address."

Sofia handed the phone to Mark. While he was talking, she said, "They may have a missing person fitting my description, but they're going to send a police car to take me to the station and to interview you and Esther about what happened."

"That's wonderful, child," Esther said, taking Sofia by the hand. "Your family will be so relieved."

"Ja," Abram agreed. He knew he should only feel relief and gladness that Sofia was finally getting the help she needed, and that now she would be able to reunite with people who cared for her. And he was glad, but he had hoped, maybe, that he would be able to see her longer, maybe ride her to the station tomorrow. Abram smiled, but his heart wasn't in it. "This is good," he said, "You'll be able see your family and rejoin your life. I hope you remember us though."

"Of course I'll remember you!" Sofia exclaimed. "How could I not? You've been so wonderful to me. All of you."

"Danki," Abram said. Mark lead then to the living room, where his two older children were relaxing, a girl of about twelve on the sofa reading by lantern-light, while her younger brother, a youth who appeared to be about nine years old, played with a wooden puzzle. They both looked up as Sofia, Esther, and Abram entered. "Gut-n-owed," the boy said, cheerfully.

Sofia and Esther sat down on the sofa beside the girl, while Abram pulled over a footstool from a chair on the opposite wall.

"Hannah, come help me attend to our guests," Mark said, waving to the girl. The girl huffed, and then carefully placing a piece of paper in between the pages of her book, followed her father towards the kitchen.

The silence that followed was awkward, the first time Abram had felt at a loss in Sofia's presence. Maybe it was Esther, seated beside Sofia on the sofa, her eyes half lidded as she leaned back on the seat. Or perhaps without the common bond of helping to protect her from danger, they had nothing in common. Especially with Sofia's memory loss. How much of what Abram felt was purely physical, the response of a man to a new face and body thrust suddenly into his life? It was safe to allow oneself to yearn for the unattainable. God may well have put Sofia into his life to open his heart again, but that didn't mean that he and Sofia had a future together.

Still, the measure of a person was not in their interests, but in their character. Was she kind? Did she care for others? Was she conscientious and diligent in her actions and thoughtful in her relationship with God? Though Abram had only known Sofia a short time, she showed evidence of being all of these things. More, everyone who met her spoke of her positively. She had walked into their community a stranger, and in less than three days, she had become dear to both Annie and Esther's family.

"You have a beautiful voice, Abram" Sofia said. "Have you studied?"

"No, but singing is an important part of our church, so I have gotten a lot of practice."

"I wish you'd had a chance to sing professionally," Sofia said. "I mean, I know your life here is more important, it's just, I think you'd do well. You have a gift."

Abram supposed he did. "I was in a band during my rumspringa, but our group broke up, and then I met Rebekah."

Abram sometimes wondered what would have happened if he hadn't met Rebekah. Would he have chosen the music instead? What would his life have been like, moving from place to place and group to group, the fast pace, hot lights, and endless worrying about money?

"What was the name of your group?" Sofia asked. "Did you ever make an album?"

"Just a single, and our drummer's brother pressed the CD's at his job after work. I think we pressed maybe 500 copies, if that. I doubt there's any left in the world."

"I wish I could hear it," Sofia said. "What was your group's name?"

"Spiral Dervish," Abram said. "Our guitarist thought it was clever."

"Spiral Dervish," Sofia said each syllable slowly, and then smiled. "I really wish I'd had a chance to know you then. I'd have been a fan."

"Danki," Abram said, his face warm more from the compliment than the heat.

Mark returned with a pitcher of iced-lemonade and Hannah carrying six cups. "To cool you off, ja," he said.

Hannah placed the cups on the end table beside the sofa and Mark poured the lemonade, which Hannah then picked up and handed out, serving Esther first. The lemonade was cool on Sofia's tongue. The boy jumped up and grabbed a cup from his sister, who drank hers at a more measured pace.

"Abram said he'd been in something called a band," the boy said. "It's for singing, and they pressed CDs. Is that some kind a bug?"

Abram laughed. "No! It's an Englischer way of storing music."

"What, they can't remember it?" the boy laughed. "Seems stupid."

"You shouldn't call people stupid," Esther said. Ice clinked in her cup. "It's not proper for a young man."

"Sorry," the boy looked down at his blocks puzzle again.

Abram had drank most of his lemonade when there was a heavy knock on the door. Abram stood, but Mark was faster, opening the door to two, uniformed police officers. One was stocky, with a shaved head and a round face with a flat, wide nose that looked like it had been broken once and set poorly. The other was thin and pale with a short beard and mustache. The thin man said, "I'm Officer Donaldson and this is Officer Michaels. Dispatch said you wanted to report an assault and battery, and that there was a woman here by the name of Sofia Angelis claiming to have amnesia who might have been declared missing, is that correct?"

"Yes," Abram said. "This way."

Both policemen had their hair buzzed very short in what seemed a uniform style. It was obvious, just by looking at them, how poorly the other two men had posed as police. The men stalking Sofia had worn uniforms two shades too dark and that fit improperly, not to mention the black club at their belt, which had been inches shorter than what these two men wore.

They walked the police officers to the living room and when the men had sat down, Officer Donaldson asked, "Which of you ladies is Sofia?"

"Me," Sofia stood. "I'm Sofia."

The cop pulled a paper from his pocket, unfolded it, and said, "Looks like her," He held it out to Sofia, "What do you think, is this you?"

"Sofia took the picture and studied it closely, "Yes...I think so...yes, it's me." She looked up, an expression of relief and joy on her face. Her fingers rested on the grainy white photo printout as she said. "It's me! It's really me!"

"Excellent, Officer Donaldson said, "Officer Michaels, will you notify the person who filed the report, we have him listed here as Daniel Havers, that we have found his fiancé?"

"Fiancé!" Sofia sounded as shocked as Abram felt. It was like a rushing river had taken root in his mind, or the static that had come over the feed when he'd finished his one, long ago, musical recording.

"You really don't remember." Officer Donaldson's face softened. "Maybe you should join Officer Michaels in the other room. It might be better if you speak with Mr. Havers yourself, after our officer has explained the situation."

"Do you know how long we've been engaged?" Sofia asked.

Officer Donaldson shook his head. "We only have what's on that printout. Mr. Havers tried to file a report three days ago when he called your Key West hotel and realized you hadn't checked in, nor had you boarded your flight last Thursday. Without evidence of foul play, though, we can't accept a missing persons report for an adult until after forty eight hours have passed. I believe Mr. Yoder attempted to inquire if there were any reports matching your description when he called last night, but it didn't hit the system until this morning."

"Oh."

"But you suspected that Ms. Angelis had been attacked, is that correct, Mr. Yoder? Why did you neglect to mention to the police that she was staying with you when you called?"

"The men who had attacked her were posing as police officers," Abram explained. "Sofia was concerned that they might have some genuine connection to your Englischer police."

"I see," Officer Donaldson said, though from the tightness of his mouth, Abram suspected he didn't. "And you waited until after your church service to report last night's incident as well."

"Abram wasn't there," Esther cut in. "Though I admit he has been right foolish, him and my Samuel. They should have called you the first time they were near a telephone and explained the whole mess. But it's all in the Lord's hands now. When there is trouble, God will make a way, as he did for us and our Sofia." She opened her palm towards Sofia. "Besides, the nastier one has been scratched by our rooster. He's got claw marks all over his hands, arms, and legs. I expect you'll be able to round him up soon enough."

"In general, it is better not to wait so long before filing a police report," Officer Donaldson said. "Be subject for the Lord's sake to every human institution, whether it be to the emperor as supreme, or to governors as sent by him to punish those who do evil and to praise those who do good."

"Peter two thirteen through twenty-five," Esther said. She folded her hands in her lap and then stared down at them. "Ja, I prayed for God to make a way, but I hadn't thought past that, as I was so wrapped up in planning the church gathering, and my son was not there to drive the buggy to Annie's. But these men are still a danger, and I am sorry for making more difficult your good works to keep our community and those around us safe. I will pray for forgiveness, and greater wisdom in the future."

"That's all anyone can ask, ma'am," the officer said. "That's all God can ask."

Sofia stood. "I suppose I need to speak with this Daniel Havers." She took a breath, and then released it slowly through her teeth. "My fiancé."

As Abram watched her go, he realized that he had lied to himself. Yes, he could bear to lose her. He had borne losing Rebekah, borne the cold space where she'd fit into his life, but even with prayer and a strong community supporting him, it hadn't been easy. Perhaps it wasn't even the loss of Sofia, but instead the certainty of more loss, that made him feel so hollow inside.

CHAPTER 5

Sofia followed Officer Donaldson to the hallway to use Annie's phone. She'd never imagined she would be engaged. Where was her ring? Probably one of the two men who had attacked her had stolen it. Sofia's borrowed shoes thudded against the hardwood floor, and her toes hurt. She glanced down again at the photograph of herself. This woman had a stylish haircut and a tank-top that bared her shoulders in a way that seemed scandalous to the woman she was now. But it wasn't the even clothes. The woman who stared out looked happy enough, but there was something artificial about it, as though she were performing for the camera. She wore a wide, straight grin, her chin lowered slightly and her face tilted to the left and her gaze was too steady, and Sofia couldn't see herself in it.

Resentment coursed through her. When Sofia got her memories back, and this woman returned, would she erase the person Sofia was becoming now? And then there was Daniel. Danny? Dan? Before her kidnapping, she had been prepared to promise her life to him, but all that she knew of him now were fragments of dreams, and none seemed meaningful: a party, a movie...what did she love about him? What was his character? Had he known that she was in danger, and more importantly, had he known why?

Instead of using Annie's phone, Officer Donaldson took a cellular phone from where it was clipped at his belt. "This is for work," he explained. "Your fiancé may not pick up a number if he doesn't recognize it, especially with everything that's going on."

"What's going on?"

"You being missing, I mean. When a young woman goes missing, it often doesn't end nearly so well. You're very lucky, Miss Angelis."

"Blessed," Sofia said. "I think I was blessed."

Officer Michaels nodded. "Can you show me the number on that report?" Sofia held the paper out to him, and using his thumb, he dialed. He held the phone to his ear as it rang, the tinny sound through the earpiece muffled, but audible where Sofia was standing. Before Officer Donaldson could speak, the voice on the other end of the line asked something, the words indistinct but the worry apparent in the voice. "No, she's fine, Mr. Havers," the officer said. "She did get into some trouble though. Apparently she was abducted and held overnight, after which she escaped and found refuge with an Amish family. She is experiencing some significant memory loss. It seems she's lost all of her memories. She was very startled when I mentioned she had a fiancé. Her ring?" Officer Michaels turned his attention to her. "Did you have a ring?" "No, nothing like that," Sofia said. "I might have lost it, or maybe it was stolen."

"She doesn't have it," the officer said. "But I'll note it in your file should it come up during the course of our investigation. Yes. Would you like to speak with Sofia now?"

Sofia's muscles were heavy with anticipation and gut twisting nervousness. Her arm shook as she took the phone and held it to her ear. "Hello?"

"Sofie?" the man on the other end said. His voice was achingly familiar. Sofia looked at the printout of the missing person's report that the officer had given her. The paper had crumpled at the left corner from where she held it so tightly. "Sofia? I was so worried! You were supposed to be in Key West." The voice of her fiancé was less welcoming than she'd imagined it would be. "What happened to Peter, your guard? Was he paid off or did these men--either way, I'm furious! They shouldn't have been able to get their hands on you."

She had a bodyguard? A man who had either sold her safety or possibly died for it? It all made Sofia feel sick and overwhelmed. "Is...is..." Her palm was so damp, the phone slid in her grip. "Are you Daniel? You're my fiancé?"

"Sofia?" his voice softened.

"I don't remember any of it," Sofia said. Not even Sofie, this affectionate nickname. Her eyes stung. She wanted to cry. "Nothing. I'm so sorry." Anything else she had to say was caught in her throat, like a thousand feathers, tickling and choking her at the same time. She rubbed her wrist under her eyes, smearing the tears over her cheeks in an attempt to dry them. "I'm sorry," she sobbed again.

"Oh, Sofie." Daniel's voice was steady, like she was a skittish horse in danger of running off. "Don't worry, we'll get this fixed. I'll have you at the best doctor in the state for memory issues come Tuesday, I promise. Do you remember anything at all?" His voice caught. "About us?"

"I remember dancing," she said. "In a beautiful room with so many people. But it's like a dream."

"Was it the ballroom with the cherry floors and chandeliers?"

"Maybe. I guess."

"That's the night I proposed," Daniel said.

For a time, they just breathed.

"Can you come here?" Sofia blurted out. "I mean, if you're coming tonight."

"Of course I'm coming tonight!" Daniel sounded angry again, and Sofia knew that the anger couldn't possibly be directed at her, but she was too raw, and he was too much of a stranger for her to easily weather the sharpness of his tone. "Where are you at exactly?"

"Annie's," Sofia realized she didn't even know her friend's last name. "I'll have her give you the address."

Officer Michaels cut in, "We'll need to take your statement at the station."

The thought of going to another place, and having to tell her threadbare story yet again to yet more strangers was overwhelming. "Can't I do it here?" Sofia asked.

"Is that the officer?" Daniel asked from the other end of the line. "May I speak with him?"

Defeated, Sofia held the phone out. "He wants to talk to you."

Daniel and the officer spoke for another minute, Officer Michaels saying the address of the station and giving directions for how to get there.

When they walked back to the living room, Annie and Abram were talking quietly in Pennsylvania Dutch. They looked up as Sofia entered.

Abram smiled, but the expression seemed a bit stiff. "I suppose with Esther along, you won't need me for this next part."

Panicked, for a moment it was as though Sofia couldn't breathe. Abram had been with her since the beginning, his presence a quiet strength that she had come to depend on. She should have been strong enough to pray, as Esther did, and know that no harm would come to her, but she wasn't. "Come," she said, her voice high and strained. "Will you please come?"

"Ja," Abram said, rubbing his hands on the thighs of his trousers. "Yes, of course. I just need to see to my horse."

"I'll take care of her," Mark said. "We'll see her nicely stabled with some nice grain, ja. You and Esther just see to our Sofia."

"Thank you!" Sofia exclaimed. She walked to him and took his hands in hers. "Thank you so much!"

Mark shook his head, "It's nothing. Just stay out of trouble, and come by and pay us a visit should you find yourself near this place again."

"I will," Sofia said, her grip tightening. "I promise. I swear, I will."

When Officer Michaels lead them to the police car, it was all Sofia could do not to run back into the house and beg Mark to let her stay. The life she was stepping back into seemed far more complicated and far more perilous than she could have imagined. But she had to confront it. She had to face the woman in the photograph, otherwise she would never know herself.

But at least, for this short time, she wouldn't have to do it alone.

CHAPTER 6

Riding in the back of the police car with its unyielding plastic seats was uncomfortable and a bit demeaning. Abram was glad he hadn't sent Sofia to face this on her own. It was difficult now, though, to sit beside her, feel the warmth of her thigh against his in the close quarters of the car, and know that she had promised herself to someone else. It seemed difficult for her as well. She kept conversation away from the future, asking first about Ruthie, and then to Esther about the cows and if they gave enough milk to sell or was it only for the family's use?

Too quickly, they had left the sheltering peace of the back roads sheltered by fields of wheat and corn to merge onto a fast moving highway. Abram often accepted rides with his furniture to various auctions or to furniture goods stores in the county, but he always found the speed and steady rumble of the car engine to feel distracting and unnatural. It felt even more so now, the blue flash from the police car painting disjointed shards of moving light in the windows and spilling in diffuse shapes on the road around them.

They gave their statements in separate rooms, after which they were allowed to rejoin each other in what seemed like another officer's office. The office had a large, cedar desk, its natural wood carved at the base of each leg. The wood had been oiled to a deep shine. Across the room from it was a large, leather sofa. When Abram returned from giving his statement, Sofia was perched on the far left side of the sofa, speaking with another woman with a sketchbook in her lap. She looked to be in her mid-fifties, with wide set brown eyes, coffee brown skin, and thick dreadlocks woven with gray and pulled back in a black hairband.

Abram glanced at the sketch as he entered the room. It was a fair likeness, Abram thought, but the chin was too short. Abram said so. The sketch artist looked up at him, fine lines fanning from the corners her narrowed eyes, and asked, "Significantly shorter? Can you describe the shape? It's always better to have more than one perspective, and you saw them in the full light of day, according to the police report."

"At least this man," Abram said, pointing to the sketch. "I only got a glimpse of the second man when I saw their car, but he never got out. He was thin and white, that's all I know."

"Yes, we're having a hard time getting a description of that one at all," the sketch artist said. "You must be Abram. Sofia has mentioned how you helped her."

"Anyone would have done the same," Abram demurred.

"Not anyone," the sketch artist said. She put the pencil down and extended her hand. "Kim," she said.

Abram shook it. Her hand was soft, and the knuckles protruded a bit, a product of years of sketching, Abram assumed. "Nice to meet you," he said. "How's it going?"

"I'm beginning to remember more though," Sofia said. "They'd worn stockings before, over their faces. I'd only have been able to identify them from voice. That's probably one of the other things that frightened me so much about them," Sofia explained. "But I think it was the third man, they called him Carl, who scared me the most. All I can remember is that he was a big man, and Kim says that may just be because he frightened me so much."

"Yes, a part of my job is to compensate for that sort of thing," Kim said. "It's perfectly understandable when someone is so frightened, that they would exaggerate certain features. He's almost certainly not as large as you think."

Sofia nodded. Abram gave more details, and while he and Sofia basically agreed, Abram disagreed on the shape of the eyes, and added the brown mole over this man Mike's left eyebrow.

The sketch was almost finished when there was a soft knock on the door. "Miss Angelis."

"Yes?" Sofia said.

"Your fiancé is here. Shall I send him in?"

Sofia's skin lost all color, and she slouched, hugging her arms over her stomach.

Kim said, "We're about finished here. I'll just give this to Officer Donaldson."

Though Abram was reluctant to leave Sofia so obviously worried, it wasn't his place to put himself between a man and his intended. "I should go."

"No!" Sofia grabbed his arm, holding it down on the table. She whispered. "Stay. Please."

"Ja," Abram said.

Sofia addressed the voice on the other side of the door. "Please, I'd like to meet him."

The door opened. A female officer came in first, followed by a handsome blond. He was tall, with a straight nose that dipped downwards slightly at the tip, a square jaw that was a touch too long, and wide, blue eyes fringed by light brown lashes. His mouth parted as his gaze fell on Sofia, and he froze, "Sofie?"

"Sofia, yes, that's me," Sofia said. "You're Daniel? Yes, you must be."

Daniel continued to stare. "Those clothes," he laughed, a weak sound that people gave when trying to cover discomfort. "You look...different, it must be the clothes. And your poor face." He raised his hand to his temple, a mirror of where the bruise sat on her face. At her continued lack of response, he said, "You really don't know me?"

"Only from my dream. I'm sorry." Sofia's fingers tightened their grip around her upper arms, and she looked ready to break. Or run. Her gaze flitted to Abram and then back to her fiancé. Abram didn't want to hate him for putting this fear and discomfort on Sofia's face. How was it that this Daniel who was ready to take vows to love and cherish this woman would stand so far away, not even offering the slightest hint of comfort?

Daniel took a step towards her, and then another. "We'll work it out," he said. "You'll get your memories back."

Sofia stood. Her shoulders and the back of her neck were tense, and while she managed a smile, it wasn't the natural, if shy expression of joy she'd given Abram when he'd driven her to Annie's house by buggy, that first day. Nor did her eyes light with the same joy she had shown after he'd sung in church. Abram knew he would hold these memories as treasures in his heart, just as he knew he had to leave her now.

"Sofia," Abram said, unwilling to inflict upon her the childish nickname that had been a part of her former life. Her future life? "It's been my honor to know you. Please, be well. Lewewohl. It means farewell."

"Abram?" Her voice caught as her gaze flitted between the two men.

Daniel said, "You're Abram? The police said you'd really gone out of your way to help my Sofie out, maybe even saved her life. There's nothing in this world that will enable me to pay you back for that."

"There's no need. We're all called by God to help each other. Love thy neighbor as thyself."

"Yes, well, we sure are lucky she arrived at your door then, aren't we Sofie," Daniel finished closing the distance between them and placed his arm around Sofia's shoulders. "Still, let me offer you something. Those guys who took her certainly were set to get a pretty penny, that's for sure." He reached into the right pocket of his black trousers and pulled out a fat envelope. "Five thousand dollars. I know you Amish don't use banks, so I took it out in cash. Please take this as the smallest token of my appreciation for how you all helped my Sofie." Sofia stood tense in his embrace as Daniel held the envelope out.

Abram looked at it, his vision blurring as fury overtook him. This man couldn't possibly be worthy of Sofia. It wasn't just the ignorance, Abram had a checking and savings account as did practically everyone he knew, or even that this Daniel offered money before even the simple courtesy of an introduction, but rather his possessive hold over Sofia and his focus on her appearance. As though her plain clothing was of equal horror to the discolored bruise on her temple.

Abram managed to keep his voice level as he said, "Again, it was Christian charity. There's no need to exact payment for simple human kindness."

"I didn't mean to offend you."

"No," Abram said, "I expect you didn't." His tone was crueler than he had right to be. "Sofia is a lovely woman, and I am grateful God brought her to me. That is all."

Sofia blinked, her eyes glistening. "Thank you," she said and haltingly added, "Denki. Gut Denki."

Abram smiled. Perfection was reserved only for God, but Sofia tried.

"They taught you some Dutch?" Daniel said, beaming a grin down upon her. "That's wonderful."

"It's German," Sofia said.

"Oh. Well, it's still great you were able to pick up some so quickly. And to think, you told me you had problems with Italian. Were you holding out on me? No, don't answer that. You wouldn't know. Have they finished up with you here do you think?"

"I should just check with Officer Donaldson," Sofia said. "And I want to say my farewells to Esther."

"The one with the powerful glare?" Daniel removed his arm from Sofia's shoulders, and instead lowered it, taking her hand in his. They started towards the door. Daniel said, "I thought she was going to take me apart. Are those shoes alright? You seem to be shuffling a little."

"I like them," Sofia said. Daniel opened the door, and Sofia went ahead of him. Daniel looked back, "Are you coming?"

"Ja," Abram said.

When the statements were made, the paperwork finished, and Abram returned to Annie's home, it was almost midnight. Over Annie and Mark's protests, Abram hitched Ruthie to the buggy and lantern in hand, urged her towards home. He was too keyed up. If he ever saw Sofia again, it seemed it would be a miracle.

The sky was clear, the moon just shy of full, and its light dimming the stars. Night insects skittered and sang as the buggy made its quiet way, and the smell of earth and growing plants filled the air. Moonlight dusted the fields and the buggy in silver. Abram had expected the heaviness he had carried these past three years to settle over him again in its stifling coat of grief, but he found himself enjoying the ride. The gentle clop of Ruthie's hooves against the pavement, the sheer emptiness of the roads, made inescapable the scale and beauty of this world that God had created. These past three years, Abram too had been traveling through his own seemingly endless night, and God's light had seemed too far and too cold to be touched. But God was as much in the stars and moon as in the sun, as much in the flutter of a moth's wings as in the brilliant display of the butterfly, and though His warmth had been difficult to feel in the long night of his grief, Abram had not been alone.

Dear God, Abram prayed, *give me the strength to remember this moment. Dear God, thank you for Rebekah, and our happiness together. Thank you for the son that Rebekah gave her life to bear, and thank you for sheltering them in your arms. And Dear God, please see Sofia through her dark night, that she may come to know herself, and through knowing herself, know your infinite love.*

Through the quiet, moon-bathed light, Abram made his way home.

CHAPTER 7

Sofia has spent two weeks in what her Amish friends would term the English world, and she feels no more comfortable amongst the trappings of her old life than she had when she arrived. For Sofia, it's like living in a dream. She and Daniel share an apartment on the second floor of a ritzy high rise condominium complex on City Avenue. They have to pass through a gate to enter, and while the doorman is very kind, as they drive down the winding street, around them towering gray buildings surrounded by islands of grass and occasional trees, it seems more of a prison than a home.

Daniel is much less abrasive once they leave the station and he is behind the wheel of his black Lexus. "Usually, I prefer something a bit less staid," he remarks when she asks about the car, "but this girl gets good mileage and she's good for the city. There's a nice 'vette in the garage though, for when we want a night on the town." He grins, a boy enamored of his toys.

The apartment Sofia and Daniel share is massive, showroom clean and completely overwhelming. Sofia walks the breadth of their living room, white carpeted, with a black leather sofa across from a wall mounted flat screen television. Speakers are mounted into the walls. There is a painting above the sofa, a modern piece that looks like a flower vase in bold purples, blues, and reds. That and the terrace, overflowing with hanging vines, flowers, and in the far corner, a container garden of tomatoes, cucumbers, and peas, are the only things that make her feel at home.

She and Daniel share a bed. It's more than large enough with a cushioning layer that molds itself to her body in a way that's both comforting and suffocating. The bedroom is wallpapered a rippling white on shimmering white, the floor a gray slate with white throw rugs at either side of the bed. Sofia sleeps on the left side. There's an e-reader on the night table. When she opens it and the machine glares brightly at her,

Daniel shows her how to use the touch screen to call up the novel she was reading, a thriller involving ghosts and a man on the run from his ex-wife. Sofia reads a few pages before shutting it.

Her parents come on the second day.

Sofia's mother Henrietta is garrulous, her hair platinum blonde and her hands flitting gold and emerald rings. The tip of her puffed hair comes to Sofia's chin, but she's loud enough for a man twice her height, and her grip is as tight as one could wish when she squeezes Sofia in a tearful hug. "We're so sorry, Sofia. Once we got out past Xi'an, they even blocked our email..." she snorts derisively, "Effing Mao, don't look so surprised, I stopped watching my tongue when you turned eighteen. But Danny said you had lost your memory. Have you gotten it back yet?"

"Little bits," Sofia says, and it's not a lie, though the recovery isn't as fast as she thought it would be. She has an appointment with a doctor the next afternoon, and she's hoping that improves things.

Her father is taller, more serious and less affectionate. He hugs her stiffly and then looking at her forehead says, "That'll fade soon, don't worry daffodil."

Sofia smiles at the nickname. She has daffodils in her garden, and their sweetness pours into the air, seeping through the deck door, which when Daniel is at work Sofia leaves open, eschewing the artificial coolness of the air conditioning for the warm breezes of the outside air.

Her parents leave after a few hours for their hotel. Sofia offers for them to stay, desperately wants them to accept, but Henrietta just laughs and says, "Oh Sofia, don't be daffy," she gives Sofia a pointed look before laughing at her own pun, and then says, "you and Daniel need your time to get reacquainted. Parents can only get in the way of some things. We'll be back tomorrow to take you to your appointment."

Every night, when Daniel returns from work, they watch television and order in. Sofia finds she enjoys Pad Thai and shrimp friend rice, but has no love of General Tso's chicken.

The appointments don't help. She's seen a psychiatrist and a psychologist and had a scan done of her brain. "Trauma induced dissociative fugue state," is the best the doctors manage. "Best to wait it out."

Daniel sleeps beside her, kisses her on the cheek in the morning and when he returns from work. He doesn't gaze at her with fire in his gaze, instead he looks at her with a desperate hope, as though every moment that passes is a fading opportunity for her to remember what they once shared. Sometimes, she wonders what it would be like to fall asleep here and wake at Abram's farm, to hear the gentle call of nature and the sweet smell of the warm morning air from the fields coming through the window. She couldn't imagine any of her friends on a bed like this one, though it is comfortable.

Sofia carefully folds the clothes and puts them on a back shelf of her closet, with Abram's wife's shoes on a shelf beneath. She tries her old clothes, stylish, low cut blouses, skinny cut jeans, dresses that whisper like cornfields as they flutter above her knees. Her closet has a mirror large enough to see herself from head to shoes. She stares at herself, the hug of how they fit and the expanses of bared flesh on her arms, chest, and legs, and she feels naked.

On the second night, Sofia asks if Daniel has a Bible. He finds one in the back of his closet, in a suitcase, a gift from his mother. Every morning, after Sofia has tended to her garden, she reads. Her parents come every afternoon. Her mother comes with a thick photo album and together, they flip through the pictures. Sofia has memorized herself as an infant, sleeping on a sheet of yellow flowers, herself as a toddler, glaring balefully at a puff of soap on her nose, and herself as a child in ballet uniform, herself as a teen, her hair a light brown wave falling to the small of her back. The memories of these experiences whisper at the edges of her mind. A cinnamon smelling Hispanic woman named Nita had taken the picture with the blocks. The one with the hair had been at a concert, and the boarding school had called her parents when she and her friends hadn't turned up for Sunday dinner. But then as soon as one memory comes clear, the others fade, and Sofia feels more and more like an outsider in her own skin.

On the third day, her best friend Terri calls from Korea, where she is teaching. Sofia has an image of her at fifteen, from the photo album. "Daniel emailed me that you were in some kind of trouble," she says, speaking like a machine gun. "What happened?"

"I was kidnapped and I lost all of my memories." Sofia says. Better to be direct, she's learned.

"Oh my God!"

"I'm sorry. I don't really remember you."

"No, it's fine. I mean, you'll get it back I'm sure. I'm just glad you're okay. Did they catch the guys?"

Sofia starts to tell the story again, but for the first time since she's come back, she's relaxed. Terri doesn't speak to her with that weight of expectation, as though every moment and every hint at remembering holds in it the keys to regaining some deep and mysterious treasure. When Sofia finishes, Terri asks, "So this Amish guy, Abram, you liked him then?"

"What?" That was the last thing Sofia had been expecting to be asked. "I mean, he was a friend."

"You don't talk about him like a friend."

"And I have Daniel."

Terri snorts, "You know how I feel about Daniel. Oh, I guess, you don't. Daniel looks good on your arm, and he's got money, but there isn't much underneath."

"He's been kind to me," Sofia says, compelled to defend the man she was supposed to love. "I don't think this is any easier for him."

"Doubt it is." Terri sighs. "Sofia, you've always done what you thought you're supposed to. You did the finance degree to make your parents happy and then you found the man that in every way ought to be perfect for you. So of course you attach yourself to him too. And Daniel's not a bad person, he's just too shallow. Always has been. I think maybe this experience has just woken you up to it."

Is Daniel shallow? Mostly he talks about his job, his vacation plans, and whatever he's watching on television, the television which is always going in the background whenever he's home. Then again, what did they have in common? Bringing up past memories would be too painful for him and too uncomfortable for her. So what can they talk about?

As Sofia's often found herself doing since she's returned, her gaze turns towards the Bible she's been reading. When Daniel gave it to her, it had still been sealed in a plastic wrapping, and the pages of fine parchment had clung together in clumps. Now some of the pages at least are beginning to have crinkles from her turning them, and the oil of her fingers is creating a faint smudge in the upper right corner.

"We should go out," Daniel suggests for their first Saturday night together. "See some of our friends. Nothing crazy," he adds, seeing her expression. "Just dinner and maybe have them back for a nightcap. Everyone's really excited to see you."

Sofia smiles and agrees, though she's ambivalent. Seeing her old friends will give her a new window into herself and herself with Daniel, but at the same time, she's nervous. She wants to feel comfortable in her old life, though she doesn't yet, and she doesn't want to embarrass her former self in front of her former friends.

They go to a fancy restaurant with two other couples. Its silk curtains and damask covered chairs, the menu is in French, and the soup spoons set horizontally above the plate. Sofia chooses her most conservative outfit, a wrap dress that exposes far too much of her chest. She puts a loose knit shawl of white and gold over it. At Daniel's prompting, she wears pearl drops from her ears and does her makeup. She's rather plain in comparison to her husband and the other couples, one a leggy blonde in heels and a wine red dress that emphasizes her lean frame.

Sofia orders something she's assured is chicken and when prompted, tells her story again. The couples gasp at appropriate moments, but are careful not to ask about her feelings. There are two men in sober black suits at a nearby table. They glance over at Sofia's group in a way that makes Sofia uncomfortable. Halfway through the salad course, Daniel whispers to her, "Stop watching the guards, you'll call attention to them."

Sofia's fork pauses, mid-bite. Methodically, she chews and swallows. She laughs when the others laugh and listens. The blonde's date, an investment banker with a dimpled chin named George asks, "So what was life like with the Amish? I bet you missed your Android."

"I didn't," Sofia says. To be honest, she doesn't use it much now. She keeps the TV off except when Daniel's home. Its chatter irritates her. And the air-conditioner, while cooling, seems false on her skin. It has no scent for her nose to savor. Yes, doing the laundry had been difficult, half by hand and the rest with the generator powered spinning washer, but she'd enjoyed the fellowship of the other girls, the conversation in the warm sun and Mary's games with the clothespins as they hung the clothes on the line. "I liked it there," Sofia adds, realizing the silence has gone too long.

George cocks his head. "I guess it's nice sometimes to get away from the fast pace of our lives."

"It wasn't slow," Sofia says. It certainly hadn't been for her, being hustled from place to place while living in constant fear of discovery. "But it was steady. There was always some kind of work, and you did it steadily, but you were never alone. There was always a sister or a friend to help."

Nothing like her days now, mostly in her apartment, tending to her flowers and occasionally taking a walk on the apartment grounds. She's ventured out of the complex twice, but the walk to the stores she'd glimpsed in the distance seemed an endless rush of beeping cars belching exhaust, their loud rumbling, and the occasional siren. She doesn't trust herself to take Daniel's expensive car out on these fast paced roads. In her loneliness, Sofia's thoughts drift to Abram, alone on his farm except for his dog, horse, and grief. But even Abram had community: sisters who made him bread, neighbors who visited, and of course his own tasks. And in his fields, it must be so much easier to feel the presence of God.

George says, "Are you an only child? I was always grateful I had my brother to play with."

Though he doesn't get what she was trying to say, Sofia smiles. She likes George, and she wonders if it would be rude to ask how they met.

When dinner is finished, Sofia closes her eyes for a brief prayer. She doesn't know why, it just seems right. She has just whispered her amen with Daniel taps his fork against the side of his flute of champagne "Excuse me," he says.

Sofia looks up to see him pull a small, velvet box from his pocket. "I wanted us all to get together not just for the chance to speak with Sofie again, but also because this is a very special day."

Sofia begins to panic. She can't possibly be expected to remember this. She wonders if maybe it's the pressure to remember that's forcing all of her memories away.

Daniel says, "When I proposed to Sofia, I had a ring specially made to suit her hand. It was lost when she was taken, but yesterday they found it in the hands of one of the men who had taken her, a Michael Maglione. It took some doing, but I've had the ring released from evidence and now..." He steps away from the table and around it, drops to one knee in front of Sofia, and opens the box.

The diamond glitter stuns Sofia's vision and she remembers. The memories sweep over her like an endless river and she can't breathe. She's an infant, in a crib, watching the shadows of the mobile inch across the ceiling. She is a toddler, following the gardener through her mother's flower garden, dragging a water pail that is almost as tall as her waist. She's a preteen, standing in front of the mirror marveling at the soreness of her chest and wondering if what grows there will be big enough to be pretty. She's a student, chatting to a handsome stranger in the chemistry lab. She's a woman, pretending to be in love. Pain shoots through Sofia's head, behind her eyes. She closes them and leans against the table, her weight on her palm.

"Sofie! What's wrong?" Daniel asks.

"I remember," Sofia says, and her cheeks are damp with tears.

Sofia's vision is too blurred to see Daniel's face, but his voice is relieved as he says, "That's wonderful! Just wonderful!" Daniel grabs her by the waist and pulls her close.

Their lips meet and Sofia is dazed. His lips are soft. Her mouth parts and he forces his tongue between her teeth. His kiss is an invasion, all tongue, saliva and movement. He smells too clean, and the sharpness of his aftershave makes her eyes water. In that moment, Sofia knows she doesn't love Daniel and she never has.

When they part, the other two couples clap.

"A toast," George shouts. "To Daniel and Sofie!"

Sofia backs away, her legs jarring against the corner of the chair. "I can't marry you," she says. "I can't."

Dear God, Sofia bows her head as Esther did, praying for guidance of any sort, *what should I do?*

In her mind, soft greens float behind her eyes. She feels the warmth of the sun, smells the sweet loam of earth, and hears the faint sound of a dog barking. There's a solid presence, holding her in a warm embrace. God is love, she remembers the verse she had just read the afternoon before. *God is love, and whoever abides in love abides in God, and God abides in him.*

"Sofie! What do you mean you can't marry me? I thought you said you remembered!"

"I'm sorry," Sofia says. How could she tell him how she had betrayed him, how the feelings she professed for him had been a well-intentioned sham.

"It's that Amish guy," Daniel says, his face flushing with fury. "What was his name, Abraham, what did you do with him?"

"Nothing," Sofia says. Nothing except fall in love.

"He kissed you?"

"No."

"Then what was it?" Daniel grabs at his hair with his left hand, holding it in a tight fist. "Why are you doing this to me?"

Sofia steps towards him and puts her hands on his shoulders. "You deserve better than the woman I was," she says, her gaze steady with his eyes. "You deserve love, as God intended."

"What's happened to you?"

Sofia wasn't sure. Transformation? Understanding? All she knew was that she was no longer a child, trying to fit herself into her adult life. Her memories had returned, and instead of shaking her faith, they had tempered it, making the steel of her belief even stronger. She couldn't stay here. She didn't want to stay. She wanted to return to the embrace of her love, and the warm acceptance of God.

It was time to go home.

CHAPTER 8

The day had dawned in cloud, wind shaking the corn on its stalks and causing Johanna to toss and growl at the foot of Abram's bed until he'd given up and awakened just after dawn. It was Saturday, and he had occasion to visit Annie's. Once Abram had shown interest in putting an advertisement in the circular to find a wife, Annie had taken it upon herself to let the entirety of Lancaster know that Abram was back on the market. Two widows from neighboring districts, and even a few of the older girls wanting to finish their rumspringa but having not yet found a mate, had responded, and if Annie had her way, Abram would be in her sitting room from morning until night until he settled on someone. Abram wasn't quite so keen, but he knew that God wanted him to fill this home with laughter and joy, and though the weight of his grief had mostly lifted, he wasn't ready to leap quite so fully into the search for a wife.

Abram ate a breakfast of leftover bread and soup, tended to the fields and to his animals, bathed and then put on his best trousers and newest shirt. He was careful not to think of Sofia, and the warmth of her smile as she admired his voice, or the way she had asked him to stay at the police station. What had Sofia done with Rebekah's shoes? Abram wondered. Had they been pushed aside to make room for her old things, or stored in a box, a hidden reminder of a nightmare best forgotten? Abram trimmed his beard and shined his shoes before donning his straw hat and hitching Ruthie to the buggy. The wind had quieted somewhat as Abram guided Ruthie onto the road. Johanna followed for a bit, barking at the buggy's heels, but Abram ordered her back and she eventually turned back to the house to sleep under the giant sycamore tree that served as the second base for his washing line.

Annie greeted him at the door. "Abram! You're early! I'm so sorry, but Sarah's youngest is ill and she can't make it today, but..."

"It's fine, ja." Was this coolness in Abram's gut relief or disappointment?

Annie's grin, perversely, seemed to grow even brighter. "Yes, but you are in luck because we have another guest who may suit you at least as well!"

"Ach, I wouldn't want to impose, especially without warning."

"You're coming in for some iced-tea, Abram Yoder," Annie said, the sternness in her tone belied by the twinkling in her eyes. Annie opened the door wide. "I was just showing my guest how I do cross-stitch in the living room, so you go in there and have a seat and I'll bring the both of you a drink."

Abram knew better than to argue with Annie on a mission, so he followed. The woman on the sofa had bowed her head as she awkwardly pushed a thick needle through a circle of white fabric. Her auburn hair was braided Amish style beneath her kapp, and she wore one of Judith's dresses. Beneath the hem peeked one of Rebekah's shoes. Sofia? It was impossible.

"Ann..." Sofia looked up and Abram's breath stopped.

"I'll just leave you two alone while I get your tea," Annie said, her voice somehow gleeful and smug at the same time.

"Abram?" Sofia stood, and the cross-stitch fell from her lap to the floor.

"I...I'll get that!" Abram managed. He crossed the space between them in five strides and dropped to his knees. She had also knelt, and their hands met as they reached for the fallen cloth.

"What brought you back?" Abram asked.

She looked up at him, her hazel eyes shining as she tightened her grip on his hand. "Love," she said. "Faith and love."

Abram returned the strength of her grip, unwilling, unable to let her go again. "I hope to know you better," he said. "If that's something you would like."

"I'd like," Sofia said with a soft smile. "I'd like that very much."

It had been so long since Abram had felt joy, pure and simple joy, that he almost didn't recognize the flutter in his heart and the lightness in his limbs. Sofia and Abram sat on the floor, fingers entwined, and talked until Annie came with the tea. Abram knew that somewhere beyond the stars, Rebekah and his son were watching, and they approved. Outside, as though teased apart by the hand of a higher power, the clouds parted and Annie's farm was bathed in light.

The End.

ABOUT THE AUTHOR

Ruth Price is a Pennsylvania native and devoted mother of four. After her youngest set off for college, she decided it was time to pursue her childhood dream to become a fiction writer. Drawing inspiration from her faith, her husband and love of her life Harold, and deep interest in Amish culture that stemmed from a childhood summer spent with her family on a Lancaster farm, Ruth began to pen the stories that had always jabbered away in her mind. Ruth believes that art at its best channels a higher good, and while she doesn't always reach that ideal, she hopes that her readers are entertained and inspired by her stories.

Feel free to learn more about Ruth Price's work at her website: www.ruthpriceauthor.com

Made in the USA
Lexington, KY
15 July 2014